Magic Cakes

KATHLEEN ROYAL PHILLIPS

Running Press
PHILADELPHIA

Running Press
Hachette Book Group
1290 Avenue of the Americas, New York, NY 10104
www.runningpress.com
@Running_Press

Printed in China

First Edition: October 2017

Published by Running Press, an imprint of Perseus Books, LLC,
a subsidiary of Hachette Book Group, Inc.

The Hachette Speakers Bureau provides a wide range of authors for speaking events.
To find out more, go to www.hachettespeakersbureau.com or call (866) 376-6591.

The publisher is not responsible for websites (or their content) that are not owned
by the publisher.

Print book cover and interior design by Amanda Richmond

Library of Congress Control Number: 2016962308
ISBNs: 978-0-7624-6305-3 (hardcover), 978-0-7624-6306-0 (ebook)

DSZN

10 9 8 7 6 5 4 3 2 1

to Mom,

for teaching me to be patient while I stirred your homemade chocolate pudding when I was only four years old—and other life lessons.

Contents

INTRODUCTION:

Making the
Magic Happen
7

~

CENTER STAGE:

Magic Cakes
19

OVER THE TOP:

Frostings, Glazes,
and Toppings

89

⌇

CURTAIN CALL

97

⌇

INDEX

98

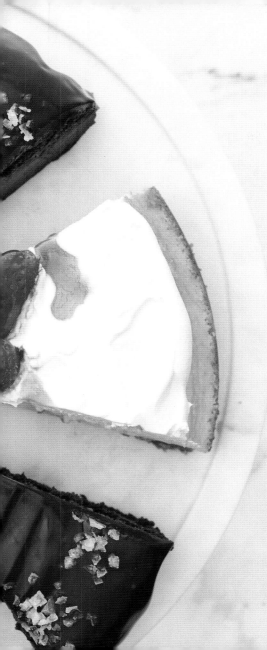

INTRODUCTION

Making the Magic Happen

One Batter. One Cake. Three Layers.

Have you ever wanted to wave your magic wand and have a fantastic dessert appear before you—or at least not have to spend hours in the kitchen preparing it? Magic cake is the answer. One thin batter goes in the oven with less than 15 minutes prep time and, magically, a three-layer cake comes out in about 40 minutes. One thick, fudge-like layer on the bottom, a creamy, silky custard middle layer, crowned with a light and spongy cake on the top: three desserts in one! From the foundational recipe Vanilla Magic Cake (page 20) to the more elaborate Salted Dark Chocolate Magic Cake (page 38), these unbelievable cakes are sure to amaze you and captivate the attention of your family and friends.

No sleight of hand here. No tricks or secret ingredients in magic cakes. The thin batter is made from staple ingredients you probably already have on hand—eggs, butter, sugar, flour, and milk. The results may look intimidating, but you won't find any difficult techniques in the making of these cakes. If you have a strong arm, you can even make them without an electric mixer with just a whisk and a couple of bowls: I opted for the mixer. The magic happens in the oven. While baking, the batter separates into three distinct layers.

The low baking temperature (325°F) allows the starch in the

flour to bind with the sugar and trap moisture from the milk, then settle to the bottom forming the dense texture of the base layer. The base layer is dense like a rich, thick blonde or chocolate brownie. Clouds of whipped egg whites coated with batter rise to the top to transform into a fluffy cake layer that is a cross between a génoise and an angel food cake. Finally, the custard layer "levitates" between the top and bottom layers. Be careful not to overcook a magic cake or this velvety layer will vanish, leaving you with only two layers. The key is to bake it just until it jiggles slightly in the center. Unlike other baked goods, you can't use a toothpick to test for doneness: it's all about the jiggle in a magic cake.

You can finish off your magic cakes simply with confectioners' sugar sprinkled on top. To gild the lily, add fruit, icings, and sauces (see page 89 for an array of toppings).

BEHIND THE SCENES

In this section, you'll find details on ingredients—how they work and best practices for handling them—and simple equipment: the baking pans, whisks, and mixers that will make all your cakes magical.

You'll notice that all of the recipes call for ingredients to be at room temperature or warmed. Bringing ingredients to lukewarm or room temperature may seem like an unnecessary step, but it does make a difference in baking: egg whites will whip higher, egg yolks and butter will trap air better, but cold milk added to a creamed butter mixture will firm the fat, hindering emulsion.

But allowing ingredients to sit on the counter to come to room temperature can take a while, keeping you from your magic cakes! Follow the tips below for each ingredient to shave a few minutes off the prep time.

EGGS: Eggs are a crucial ingredient in cakes in general and have a dual role in magic cakes. Egg yolks help moisten the bottom layer and thicken the custard layer. The eggs and sugar are beaten together for several minutes to incorporate sugar crystals into the mixture. This creates air bubbles in the batter. The air bubbles expand during baking, lifting the batter, which causes the cake to rise.

I was curious about how the magic cake batter would fare with the egg yolk mixture whisked by hand versus with an electric mixer, so I performed a side-by-side test with two identical cakes, whisking the egg yolks and sugar for 2 minutes by hand for one cake (I got my upper body workout!) and beating the second one with an electric hand mixer for 2 minutes. Both mixtures became light in color, although the second mixture was lighter (closer to lemon colored). Although both mixtures turned out acceptable cakes, the one beaten with the mixer had a taller sponge cake and slightly less dense bottom layer. Your takeaway is this: it is important to beat the eggs yolks and sugar together at least 2 minutes in these recipes, preferably with a mixer. Set a timer to make things easy. I didn't even attempt to whisk the egg whites by hand. Unless you have some serious arm muscles and for the best overall cake results, go electric.

The egg whites form the structure of the sponge cake layer. When egg whites are beaten into a foam that forms stiff peaks, tiny air bubbles are trapped and the egg whites multiply in volume up to eight times. For maximum volume, start with room-temperature eggs. Separate the yolk from the white carefully. One tiny drop of egg yolk or fat in the whites can deflate them or prevent them from whipping altogether. Avoid using plastic bowls for beating the egg whites; they tend to trap fat. Acid, such as cream of tartar, vinegar, or lemon juice, is used to help stabilize and increase the volume of the egg whites. I prefer cream of tartar over vinegar or lemon juice, especially when using large amounts of egg whites in recipes, because of the extra liquid they add to the foam. Cream of tartar also does a better job of preventing the egg whites from overbeating. The typical ratio of cream of tartar is $1/8$ teaspoon per egg white.

It takes at least 30 minutes for refrigerated eggs sitting on the counter to reach room temperature. It's like watching paint dry. If you separate them first, then let them come to room temperature, you can shave off a few minutes. But the quickest way to bring them to room temperature is to place the whole eggs in a small, deep bowl and pour warm, not hot, water over them and let them stand for 5 minutes. All eggs used in magic cakes are grade A large.

BUTTER: Most every pastry textbook will tell you that unsalted butter is best in cakes and desserts so you can control the amount of salt by adding your own. While this is true, I have found after testing and retesting more than forty magic cakes that salted butter contains just the right amount of salt for my taste without having to add another ingredient. I even love salted butter in the peanut butter cake. If you prefer less salt or have unsalted butter on hand, then it is perfectly fine to use what you have and adjust accordingly. Again, one of the beautiful things about magic cakes is that you can make them from what you already have in your pantry and refrigerator.

My trick for melting butter is to cut one stick of butter into four pieces and place in a small microwave-safe bowl or measuring cup. Save the paper wrapper and place it on the top of the bowl to prevent any splattering in the microwave. Microwave on HIGH for thirty seconds, and you have perfectly melted butter; it's not too hot so you don't have to wait for it to cool down. My microwave is 1,200 watts; yours may need another fifteen-second burst if the wattage is lower.

SUGAR: Sugar does more than sweeten. Not only does it help moisten the bottom layer, it tenderizes the sponge cake layer and prevents it from drying out.

FLOUR: You can add as much as 2 tablespoons per cup too much to a recipe if you measure incorrectly. First, stir the flour in the canister with a dry whisk before measuring to loosen the flour. Lightly spoon the flour into dry measuring cups and level it off with a table knife. Avoid scooping the measuring cup right into the flour canister; this packs in extra flour.

MILK: The milk is whole unless otherwise indicated. When developing these recipes, I sometimes changed the milk according to the nature of the recipe. For example, sweet potato pies typically use evaporated milk, so I used a can of evaporated milk, which equals $1\frac{3}{4}$ cups, in Cardamom Sweet Potato Magic Cake with Chantilly Cream (page 44). Since the recipe needs a total of 2 cups, I just made up the difference with $\frac{1}{4}$ cup whole milk I had in my fridge rather than opening another can of evaporated milk for such a small amount. For Coconut-Chocolate Magic Cake Bars (page 82), I used canned coconut milk. My first test with refrigerated coconut milk beverage was a fail due to the high water content in this "milk." The carton is for drinking; the can is for cooking.

When I see the words "lukewarm milk" in a recipe, I cringe just a little for fear someone, in an effort to reach lukewarm, might leave milk out at room temperature for too long. Based on my catering experience, I know that milk left out too long could possibly be in the danger zone of 40° to 140°F. To avoid this, microwave 2 cups of cold milk on HIGH for 1 minute and be done with it.

PANS: Most of the magic cake recipes you see posted on the Internet are prepared in square or round cake pans. To that standard equipment, I've added springform pans, jumbo muffin pans, loaf pans, and silicone pans and liners. If a recipe includes add-ins, such as fruit or cookies, which increase the volume in the pan, I may suggest increasing the size of the pan from 8 to 9 inches, but the basic recipes are prepared in 8-inch pans. Eight-inch springform pans are often found in a graduated set of pans. Meyer Lemon Magic Cake Bars (page 77) is made in a 13 x 9 x 2-inch baking pan. When I prepare traditional lemon bars, I'm usually making them for an occasion that demands more than twelve bars, so I start by almost doubling the basic Vanilla Magic Cake (page 20) recipe and go from there to serve a crowd.

For all round cake pans, I recommend using a springform pan because the removable sides make it easier to transfer the cake to a

serving plate; plus they have higher sides, which can hold 8 to 9 cups of batter. Be sure to check a spring-form pan for leaks. Simply fill it with tap water before using. If it leaks, wrap the outside of the pan with aluminum foil. This is an old cheesecake-baking trick. Lining a regular cake pan with aluminum foil or parchment paper will also help remove the cake from the pan if you don't have a springform pan. Make sure the foil and parchment over-hang by about 2 inches to use as handles to remove the cake from the pan. You don't have to purchase a new pan if you already have a regu-lar 8- or 9-inch cake pan, but be sure the cake pans have at least 2-inch sides. You can extend the height of the sides of a pan by using a large piece of aluminum foil to line the pan and shaping the overhang upward to form higher sides.

Lining the regular pans with alumi-num foil or parchment is not neces-sary for the success of a magic cake, but it is extremely helpful when removing the cake from a pan that doesn't have removable sides. I prefer aluminum foil to parchment paper to line round pans because the aluminum foil can be pressed almost flat against the pan to take on the shape of the pan; parchment tends to create folds, which are baked into the sides of the cake. I fell in love with silicone pans of all shapes. When the cake is chilled, you can either pull back the sides of the pan and push up on the bottom as you slide the cake onto a serving plate with the help of a metal spat-ula, or turn the pan upside down on the plate and pull back on the sides. Be sure to place a silicone pan on a baking sheet first before putting it in the oven: it is nearly impossible to transfer the pan to the oven without it bending inward, full of the thin batter . . . trust me on this one.

Glass and ceramic dishes can be used for magic cakes, but they are not ideal, especially glass. Glass is not a good conductor of heat, so it takes a little longer to heat up than metal. Once hot—and it can get very hot—it takes much longer to cool down, causing the cake to continue to cook slightly, which could affect the creaminess of the custard layer. If you do use glass or ceramic pans, reduce the oven temperature by 25°F and possibly bake 5 minutes less, still giving it the jiggle test.

MIXER: An electric mixer comes in handy when beating the egg whites for 2 minutes. The egg yolks will almost achieve the lemon-colored look with just a wire whisk, but my best results were with a mixer because of the amount of air it can incorporate (see page 10 for more details about the side-by-side comparison). I initially tried making several magic cakes using one hand mixer for the entire recipe. By washing the beaters thoroughly in between beating the batter with the egg yolks in one bowl and the egg whites in a separate bowl—to ensure that no fat from the batter encountered the whites—I achieved excellent results. I then tested most of the remaining recipes using both a stand mixer and a hand mixer. While the egg yolks were beating for 2 minutes in the stand mixer, I beat the egg whites in a separate bowl with the hand mixer. Though using both is not crucial, if you do have a stand mixer and hand mixer, it will provide added insurance and speed up the cake making. One of the "magical" things about magic cakes is that they seem to defy the traditional laws of cake-baking science, one of which states that egg yolks and sugar must be beaten for a long time; many sponge cake recipes recommend beating the eggs and sugar for at least 3 to 5 minutes—versus the 2 minutes needed for magic cakes. But then, these are not ordinary cakes.

BAKING AND STORAGE

Magic cakes are incredibly easy desserts. The most challenging step is determining the jiggle in the cake when baking: too much jiggle and you end up spooning it out of the pan instead of slicing it; not enough jiggle and the custard layer disappears. The right amount of jiggle is similar to the jiggle you see when baking a cheesecake, with just a little less jiggle in the center. The 1 to 2 inches across the very middle should jiggle like Jell-O, not slosh like thin batter.

In order to achieve the right amount of jiggle in the center, baking times will vary slightly depending on the ingredients used, thickness of the pan, and accuracy of the oven. Thicker pans will require a longer baking time. An inexpensive oven thermometer will determine if your oven is accurate and help you achieve the right amount of jiggle in just the right amount of time.

Magic cakes can be covered and refrigerated up to three days.

CREATE YOUR OWN MAGIC

My wish is to inspire you to conjure up some of your own magic. You can design your own magic-cake creation by thinking of your favorite three-layer cake, cheesecake, dessert, or cookie and go from there. Let's say German chocolate cake is your all-time favorite cake. Here's how you can create a German chocolate magic cake using Chocolate Magic Cake (page 23) as your base recipe. Melt 2 ounces of chopped Baker's German's Sweet Chocolate with $1/4$ cup of milk. Stir in $1/2$ cup toasted chopped pecans and $1/2$ cup sweetened flaked coconut and then fold in egg whites. Spread this mixture in the bottom of an 8-inch springform pan and pour batter over it. Drizzle Ganache Glaze made with dark chocolate (page 95) over the baked cake and garnish with toasted coconut and pecan halves. Voilà! German chocolate magic cake. Almost any dessert lends itself to the magic cake treatment, with a little ingenuity. (I have actually tested this recipe, and it was full of yum factor; there just wasn't enough room in the book to include all the flavor combinations that flooded my imagination.) Many of these magic cakes are actually hybrid desserts. For example, Coconut Cream Magic Cake (page 29) combines a three-layer coconut cake with coconut cream pie.

Presto! Now, you have the behind-the-scenes scoop. You don't have to be a Houdini in your own kitchen to impress your audience (aka, your family and friends) with these simple, yet remarkable recipes in *Magic Cakes*.

CENTER STAGE:
Magic Cakes

Vanilla Magic Cake

Makes 9 servings

The mother of all magic cakes, this recipe is the foundation from which all the recipes in this cook-book were developed. The sugar can be changed to light- or dark-brown sugar, maple syrup, honey, or molasses. Coconut milk, evaporated milk, and half-and-half can be traded in for whole milk. Flavorings and add-ins, such as fruit, cookies, and nuts, can be stirred in. And finally, you can top it off (or gild the lily so to speak) with glazes, whipped cream, and caramel sauce (see page 96). Even unadorned, this cake is still magical with its three contrasting vanilla layers.

4 large eggs, at room temperature	¾ cup all-purpose flour
¾ cup granulated sugar	2 cups lukewarm whole milk
½ cup (1 stick) salted butter, melted	½ teaspoon cream of tartar
1 teaspoon vanilla extract	1 teaspoon confectioners' sugar

Preheat oven to 325°F. Line an 8-inch square cake pan with aluminum foil or parchment paper, allowing 2 inches of overhang around the sides; coat with baking spray.

Separate the eggs; place the egg yolks in a mixing bowl with the sugar and beat on high speed with an electric mixer for 2 minutes, or until lemon colored. On low speed, gradually add the melted butter and vanilla, scraping down sides as needed. Add the flour and mix just until flour is combined. Gradually add the milk, beating just until combined.

If using the same mixer and beaters to beat the egg whites, wash the beaters thoroughly; place the egg whites in a separate mixing bowl. Beat on medium speed until foamy; add cream of tartar. Increase the speed to high and beat until the egg whites form stiff peaks, about 2 minutes. Gently whisk about one-third of the egg whites into the thin batter; gently fold the remaining egg whites in with a silicone spatula. Pour the batter in the prepared cake pan. (The pan will be almost full.) Bake for 40 minutes, or until the center jiggles slightly when gently shaken.

Let cool completely on a wire rack, about 1 hour. Cover and refrigerate at least 2 hours to chill. Remove the cake from the pan using aluminum foil as handles. Remove foil and transfer the cake to a serving plate. Sprinkle with confectioners' sugar using a fine mesh sieve or sifter.

Chocolate Magic Cake

Makes 9 servings

Decadent on its own or as a blank canvas for other creative flavors, such as red velvet, German chocolate, or mocha latte, this cake is sure to satisfy your chocolate craving.

4 large eggs, at room temperature
¾ cup granulated sugar
½ cup (1 stick) salted butter, melted
1 teaspoon vanilla extract
½ cup all-purpose flour

⅓ cup unsweetened cocoa
2 cups lukewarm whole milk
½ teaspoon cream of tartar
1 teaspoon confectioners' sugar
   or unsweetened cocoa

Preheat oven to 325°F. Line an 8-inch square cake pan with aluminum foil or parchment paper, allowing 2 inches of overhang around the sides; coat with baking spray.

Separate the eggs; place the egg yolks in a mixing bowl with the sugar and beat on high speed with an electric mixer for 2 minutes, or until lemon colored. On low speed, gradually add the melted butter and vanilla, scraping down sides as needed. Add the flour and cocoa. Mix just until flour is combined. Gradually add the milk, beating just until combined.

If using the same mixer and beaters to beat the egg whites, wash the beaters thoroughly. Place the egg whites in a separate mixing bowl. Beat on medium speed until foamy; add cream of tartar. Increase the speed to high and beat until the egg whites form stiff peaks, about 2 minutes. Gently whisk about one-third of the egg whites into the thin batter; gently fold the remaining egg whites in with a silicone spatula. Pour the batter in the prepared cake pan. (The pan will be almost full.) Bake for 40 minutes, or until the center jiggles slightly when gently shaken.

Let cool completely on a wire rack, about 1 hour. Cover and refrigerate at least 2 hours to chill. Remove the cake from the pan using aluminum foil as handles. Remove foil and transfer the cake to a serving plate. Sprinkle with confectioners' sugar or cocoa.

Note: **You can easily make a red velvet magic cake by adding 2 teaspoons red food coloring. Then, serve it side by side with Purple Velvet Magic Cake (page 40)!**

Key Lime Magic Cake

Makes 9 servings

This cake hits the spot for those who prefer the light and tangy flavor of citrus to rich, intense chocolate. Any freshly squeezed citrus can be substituted: tangerine, blood orange, Meyer lemon, or grapefruit. I baked one with orange juice, and it reminded me of the Creamsicle ice-cream pops I loved as a kid.

4 large eggs, at room temperature
¾ cup granulated sugar
½ cup (1 stick) salted butter, melted
1 teaspoon vanilla extract
¾ cup all-purpose flour
1¾ cups lukewarm whole milk
2 teaspoons freshly grated key lime zest

⅓ cup freshly squeezed key lime juice
½ teaspoon cream of tartar
1 recipe Sweetened Whipped Cream
  (page 91)
Fresh lime slices, for garnish
¼ cup sweetened shredded dried coconut,
  for garnish (optional)

Preheat oven to 325°F. Line an 8-inch square cake pan with aluminum foil or parchment paper, allowing 2 inches of overhang around the sides; coat with baking spray.

Separate the eggs; place the egg yolks in a mixing bowl with the sugar and beat on high speed with an electric mixer for 2 minutes, until lemon colored. On low speed, gradually add the melted butter and vanilla, scraping down sides as needed. Add the flour and mix just until flour is combined. Gradually add the milk, zest, and lime juice, beating just until combined.

If using the same mixer and beaters to beat the egg whites, wash the beaters thoroughly; place the egg whites in a separate mixing bowl.

Beat on medium speed until foamy; add cream of tartar. Increase the speed to high and beat until the egg whites form stiff peaks, about 2 minutes. Gently whisk about one-third of the egg whites into the thin batter; gently fold the remaining egg whites in with a silicone spatula. Pour the batter in the prepared cake pan. (The pan will be almost full.) Bake for 35 minutes, or until the center jiggles slightly when gently shaken.

Let cool completely on a wire rack, about 1 hour. Cover and refrigerate at least 2 hours to chill. Remove the cake from the pan using aluminum foil as handles. Remove foil and transfer the cake to a serving plate. Spread

Sweetened Whipped Cream over the top of the cake; garnish with lime slices and coconut.

Notes: **It's easier to first remove zest from a whole lime before cutting it in half to juice it. This cake requires less baking time because the acid in the lime juice starts "cooking" or denaturing the proteins of the eggs immediately.**

Gingerbread Magic Cake with Orange Curd

Makes 9 servings

Gingerbread not only ranks high on my list of favorite fall treats to eat, it's also number one on my list to bake—just so I can smell the warm spices of ginger, cinnamon, and cloves wafting throughout the house. Getting to actually eat this moist, molasses-infused cake is an added bonus. #smells betterthanacandle

4 large eggs, at room temperature
⅔ cup firmly packed light-brown sugar
½ cup (1 stick) salted butter, melted
¼ cup unsulfured molasses
1 teaspoon vanilla extract
¾ cup all-purpose flour
2 teaspoons ground ginger
1 teaspoon ground cinnamon

⅛ teaspoon ground cloves
2 cups lukewarm whole milk
½ teaspoon cream of tartar
1 (10-ounce) jar orange or lemon curd (1 cup)
1 cup crème fraîche or whipped cream (optional)
2 teaspoons freshly grated orange or lemon zest, for garnish

Preheat oven to 325°F. Line an 8-inch square cake pan with aluminum foil or parchment paper, allowing 2 inches of overhang around the sides; coat with baking spray.

Separate the eggs; place the egg yolks in a mixing bowl with the sugar and beat on high speed with an electric mixer for 2 minutes, or until lighter in color. On low speed, gradually add the melted butter, molasses, and vanilla, scraping down sides as needed. Combine flour and spices; add to butter mixture just until flour mixture is combined. Gradually add the milk, beating just until combined.

If using the same mixer and beaters to beat the egg whites, wash the beaters thoroughly; place the egg whites in a separate mixing bowl. Beat on medium speed until foamy; add cream of tartar. Increase the speed to high and beat until the egg whites form stiff peaks, about 2 minutes. Gently whisk about one-third of the egg whites into the thin batter; gently fold the remaining egg whites in with a silicone spatula. Pour the batter in the prepared cake pan. (The pan will be almost full.) Bake for 30 to

35 minutes, or until the center jiggles slightly when gently shaken.

Let cool completely on a wire rack, about 1 hour. Cover and refrigerate at least 2 hours to chill. Remove the cake from the pan using aluminum foil as handles. Remove foil and transfer the cake to a serving plate.

Spoon orange or lemon curd into a small microwave-safe bowl. Microwave orange or lemon curd, uncovered, on HIGH for 30 seconds or until thin enough to drizzle. Drizzle the warm curd over the cake, allowing it to drip over the sides. Cut into squares; dollop with crème fraîche or whipped cream, if desired. Garnish with orange or lemon zest.

Coconut Cream Magic Cake

Makes 10 servings

This hybrid recipe contains two of Grandma's quintessential holiday recipes in one: three-layer coconut cake with marshmallow-like frosting and coconut cream pie with a creamy, custard filling, topped with mounds of flaked or shaved coconut. I call this marshmallow frosting Six-Minute Frosting because it takes even less time to make than the traditional 7-minute frosting. This is a generous amount of frosting, so don't be afraid to mound it high on top of the cake, or you can also frost the sides.

4 large eggs, at room temperature
¾ cup granulated sugar
½ cup (1 stick) salted butter, melted
1 teaspoon vanilla extract
¾ cup all-purpose flour
1½ cups whole milk

½ cup canned coconut milk
½ teaspoon cream of tartar
1 recipe Six-Minute Frosting (page 90)
¾ cup large shredded unsweetened
 dried coconut

Preheat oven to 325°F. Coat an 8-inch spring-form pan with baking spray or line an 8-inch round cake pan with aluminum foil, allowing 2 inches of overhang around the sides, and coat with baking spray.

Separate the eggs; place the egg yolks in a mixing bowl with the sugar and beat on high speed with an electric mixer for 2 minutes, or until lemon colored. On low speed, gradually add the melted butter and vanilla, scraping down sides as needed. Add the flour and mix just until flour is combined. Gradually add both milks, beating just until combined.

If using the same mixer and beaters to beat the egg whites, wash the beaters thoroughly; place the egg whites in a separate mixing bowl. Beat on medium speed until foamy; add cream of tartar. Increase the speed to high and beat

until the egg whites form stiff peaks, about 2 minutes. Gently whisk about one-third of the egg whites into the thin batter; gently fold the remaining egg whites in with a silicone spatula. Pour the batter in the prepared cake pan. (The pan will be almost full.) Bake for 38 to 40 minutes, or until the center jiggles slightly when gently shaken.

Let cool completely on a wire rack, about 1 hour. Cover and refrigerate at least 2 hours to chill. If using a springform pan, remove sides and bottom of pan; otherwise, remove the cake from the pan using aluminum foil as handles. Remove foil and transfer the cake to a serving plate.

Spread Six-Minute Frosting over the top of the cake and sprinkle generously with coconut. Cover and refrigerate at least 30 minutes for frosting to set, or until ready to serve.

Banana Pudding Magic Cake

Makes 9 servings

Meringue or whipped cream on banana pudding? Most people prefer one or the other—strongly. I'm a whipped cream fan, but my husband prefers meringue; neither of us would turn down banana pudding either way. It has to be among the top five ultimate comfort desserts—at least in the South— so of course, I've included a banana pudding version of the magic cake. If you are a die-hard meringue fan, you could dollop an Italian meringue on the cake and use a kitchen torch to brown the edges.

2 medium-size ripe bananas, divided
4 large eggs, at room temperature
¾ cup granulated sugar
½ cup (1 stick) salted butter, melted
1 teaspoon vanilla extract
¾ cup all-purpose flour

1 (12-ounce) can evaporated milk
½ cup lukewarm whole milk
½ teaspoon cream of tartar
1 recipe Sweetened Whipped Cream (page 91)
¾ cup mini vanilla-flavored wafer cookies, crumbled (like Nilla Wafers)

Preheat the oven to 325°F. Line an 8-inch square cake pan with aluminum foil or parchment paper, allowing 2 inches of overhang around the sides; coat with baking spray.

Mash 1 of the bananas: you should have about ½ cup mashed banana.

Separate the eggs; place the egg yolks in a mixing bowl with the sugar and beat on high speed with an electric mixer for 2 minutes, or until lemon colored. On low speed, gradually add the melted butter, mashed banana, and vanilla, scraping down the sides as needed. Add the flour and mix just until flour is combined. Gradually add both milks, beating just until combined.

If using the same mixer and beaters to beat the egg whites, wash the beaters thoroughly; place the egg whites in a separate mixing bowl.

Beat on medium speed until foamy; add the cream of tartar. Increase the speed to high and beat until the egg whites form stiff peaks, about 2 minutes. Gently whisk about one-third of the egg whites into the thin batter; gently fold the remaining egg whites in with a silicone spatula. Pour the batter in the prepared cake pan. (The pan will be almost full.) Bake for 40 minutes, or until the center jiggles slightly when gently shaken.

Let cool completely on a wire rack, about 1 hour. Cover and refrigerate at least 2 hours to chill. Remove the cake from the pan using aluminum foil as handles. Remove foil and transfer the cake to a serving plate.

Spread or dollop Sweetened Whipped Cream on top of the cake. Slice the remaining banana and garnish the cake with banana slices and cookies.

Cranberry-Orange Magic Cake

Makes 9 servings

Clafoutis is an easy French dessert made by pouring a pancake-like batter over fruit, most commonly cherries, and baking it. Sound familiar? It's not too far off from our own magic cakes. Although magic cakes are typically served chilled, I tried this one warm because it reminded me of the fruit-topped dessert, and I loved the pudding-like texture the middle layer takes on before chilling. The fruit possibilities are only limited by what's in season: blueberries, cranberries, raspberries, pears, strawberries, figs, and plums.

1¼ cups fresh cranberries, divided
4 large eggs, at room temperature
¾ cup granulated sugar
½ cup (1 stick) salted butter, melted
2 teaspoons freshly grated orange zest, divided
1 teaspoon vanilla extract

½ cup all-purpose flour
¼ cup almond flour or finely ground blanched almonds
2 cups lukewarm half-and-half
½ teaspoon cream of tartar
1 teaspoon confectioners' sugar

Preheat the oven to 325°F. Butter an 8- to 9-inch square or round cast-iron skillet. My square skillet is 8½ inches. Spread 1 cup of the cranberries in bottom of skillet.

Separate the eggs; place the egg yolks in a mixing bowl with the sugar and beat on high speed with an electric mixer for 2 minutes, or until lemon colored. On low speed, gradually add the melted butter, 1 teaspoon orange zest, and vanilla, scraping down the sides as needed. Add the flours and mix just until flour is combined. Gradually add the half-and-half, beating just until combined.

If using the same mixer and beaters to beat the egg whites, wash the beaters thoroughly; place the egg whites in a separate mixing bowl. Beat on medium speed until foamy; add the cream of tartar. Increase the speed to high and beat until the egg whites form stiff peaks, about

2 minutes. Gently whisk about one-third of the egg whites into the thin batter; gently fold the remaining egg whites in with a silicone spatula. Pour the batter over the cranberries in the prepared skillet. (An 8½-inch skillet will be almost full.) Bake 15 minutes. Without moving the pan, sprinkle the remaining ¼ cup cranberries on top of the cake. The cake will not fall but allow the cranberries to suspend on top of the cake. Bake for 20 to 25 more minutes, or until the center jiggles slightly when gently shaken.

Let cool 30 minutes on a wire rack. The cake will still be warm, but it will firm up just enough so that it's easier to cut or spoon out. Sprinkle remaining orange zest and confectioners' sugar over the cake. Serve the cake warm or at room temperature in the cast-iron skillet or cover and chill 2 hours, to serve chilled.

Magical Confetti Birthday Cake

Makes 10 servings

Add some colorful razzle-dazzle to the party with this magic cake. Multicolor sprinkles both inside and out with sparkler cake candles on the top will produce oohs and aahs at your next birthday party.

4 large eggs, at room temperature
¾ cup granulated sugar
½ cup (1 stick) salted butter, melted
1 teaspoon vanilla extract
¾ cup all-purpose flour
2 cups lukewarm whole milk
½ teaspoon cream of tartar

3 tablespoons rainbow sprinkles, plus
  2 tablespoons for garnish
1 recipe Vanilla Icing (page 92)
1 tablespoon white sparkling sugar,
  for garnish (optional)
½ teaspoon edible glitter, for garnish (optional)
Cake sparklers or sparkler candles

Preheat oven to 325°F. Coat an 8-inch spring-form pan with baking spray or line an 8-inch round cake pan with aluminum foil, allowing 2 inches of overhang around the sides, and coat with baking spray.

Separate the eggs; place the egg yolks in a mixing bowl with the sugar and beat on high speed with an electric mixer for 2 minutes, or until lemon colored. On low speed, gradually add the melted butter and vanilla, scraping down sides as needed. Add the flour and mix just until flour is combined. Gradually add the milk, beating just until flour is combined.

If using the same mixer and beaters to beat the egg whites, wash the beaters thoroughly; place the egg whites in a separate mixing bowl. Beat on medium speed until foamy; add cream of tartar. Increase the speed to high and beat until the egg whites form stiff peaks, about 2 minutes. Gently whisk about one-third of the egg whites into the thin batter; gently fold in

the remaining egg whites and 3 tablespoons of sprinkles with a silicone spatula. (The pan will be almost full.) Bake for 40 minutes, or until the center jiggles slightly when gently shaken.

Let cool completely on a wire rack, about 1 hour. Cover and refrigerate at least 2 hours to chill. If using a springform pan, remove sides and bottom of pan; otherwise, remove the cake from the pan using aluminum foil as handles. Remove foil and transfer the cake to a serving plate. Spread Vanilla Icing over the cake, allowing icing to drip over the edges. Sprinkle remaining 2 tablespoons of sprinkles, the sparkling sugar, and edible glitter over the cake, and place cake sparklers or candles in the center of the cake.

Note: **Cake sparklers are not the same as fireworks sparklers. They do not contain magnesium, chlorates, or perchlorates and can easily be found online.**

Magic Sticky Toffee Puddings

Makes 9 servings

These mini cakes have all the gooey, rich flavors of traditional sticky toffee pudding with an added bonus layer of custard. Unlike most magic cakes, these cakes beg to be served warm, with a dollop of whipped cream or vanilla ice cream on each one.

1 (8-ounce) package dried chopped dates
½ teaspoon baking soda
4 large eggs, at room temperature
½ cup firmly packed dark-brown sugar
½ cup (1 stick) salted butter, melted
¼ cup unsulfured molasses

1 teaspoon vanilla extract
1 teaspoon freshly grated orange zest
¾ cup all-purpose flour
2 cups lukewarm half-and-half
½ teaspoon cream of tartar
1 recipe Toffee Sauce (page 93)

Preheat the oven to 325°F. Coat 9 jumbo muffin pans or jumbo silicone cupcake liners with baking spray. If using liners, place them on a baking sheet.

Combine dates and ¾ cup water in a small saucepan; bring to a boil over medium heat. Cook 2 minutes, stirring often. Turn off the heat and stir in the baking soda. Let stand 10 minutes to soften the dates.

Separate the eggs; place the egg yolks in a mixing bowl with the sugar and beat on high speed with an electric mixer for 2 minutes, or until lighter in color. On low speed, gradually add the melted butter, molasses, vanilla, and orange zest, scraping down sides as needed. Add the flour and mix just until flour is combined. Gradually add the half-and-half, beating just until combined. Add softened dates and any soaking liquid, beating on low just until combined.

If using the same mixer and beaters to beat the egg whites, wash the beaters thoroughly; place the egg whites in a separate mixing bowl.

Beat on medium speed until foamy; add cream of tartar. Increase the speed to high and beat until the egg whites form stiff peaks, about 2 minutes. Gently whisk about one-third of the egg whites into the thin batter; gently fold the remaining egg whites in with a silicone spatula. Pour batter evenly in prepared muffin pans, filling almost full. Bake for 15 to 18 minutes, or until the centers barely jiggle when gently shaken.

Let cool completely on a wire rack, about 45 minutes. Cover and refrigerate at least 1½ hours to chill. Run a butter knife around outside edges of muffin pans; carefully remove cakes from pans or silicone liners to serving plates. Serve with Toffee Sauce.

Notes: **Baking soda is added to dried dates to help soften them.**

Regular-size muffin pans and silicone liners will not work as well because they are not deep enough to make the three distinct layers.

Salted Dark Chocolate Magic Cake

Makes 10 servings

All things chocolate go into this decadent cake: dark chocolate, chocolate milk, Dutch-processed cocoa, and Dark Chocolate Ganache Glaze (page 95). Adding strong coffee intensifies the rich chocolate flavor of this cake. The velvety smooth ganache is contrasted by the crunchy, delicate flakes of Maldon sea salt.

1 tablespoon instant espresso powder
½ cup dark chocolate chips (53 to 60% cacao)
2 cups lukewarm chocolate whole milk, divided
4 large eggs, at room temperature
¾ cup granulated sugar
½ cup (1 stick) salted butter, melted
1 teaspoon vanilla extract

½ cup all-purpose flour
¼ cup dark Dutch-processed cocoa
  (I use Hershey's Cocoa Special Dark)
½ teaspoon cream of tartar
1 recipe Dark Chocolate Ganache Glaze
  (page 95)
¾ teaspoon flaked Maldon sea salt

Preheat oven to 325°F. Coat an 8-inch springform pan with baking spray or line an 8-inch round cake pan with aluminum foil, allowing 2 inches of overhang around the sides, and coat with baking spray.

Stir together espresso powder and 2 teaspoons hot water in a small bowl or a custard cup. Combine chocolate chips and ¼ cup chocolate milk in a 1-cup glass measuring cup. Microwave on HIGH for 30 seconds; stir well. Microwave on HIGH for 15 seconds, if necessary; stir until smooth.

Separate the eggs; place the egg yolks in a mixing bowl with the sugar and beat on high speed with an electric mixer for 2 minutes, or until lemon colored. On low speed, gradually add the melted butter and vanilla, scraping down sides as needed.

Add espresso and melted chocolate and beat just until combined on medium speed. On low speed, add the flour and cocoa; beat just until flour is combined. Gradually add remaining 1¾ cups chocolate milk, beating just until combined.

If using the same mixer and beaters to beat the egg whites, wash the beaters thoroughly; place the egg whites in a separate mixing bowl. Beat on medium speed until foamy; add cream of tartar.

Increase the speed to high and beat until the egg whites form stiff peaks, about 2 minutes. Gently whisk about one-third of the egg whites into the thin batter; gently fold the remaining egg whites in with a silicone spatula. Pour the

batter in the prepared cake pan. Bake for 40 minutes, or until the center jiggles slightly when gently shaken.

Let cool completely on a wire rack, about 1 hour. Cover and refrigerate at least 2 hours to chill. If using a springform pan, remove sides and bottom of pan; otherwise, remove the cake from the pan using aluminum foil as handles. Remove foil and transfer the cake to a serving plate.

Spread the glaze on top of the cake, allowing it to drip over the sides. Place cake in the refrigerator 10 minutes or until ganache is set. Sprinkle the salt along the outside edges of the cake.

Note: **For Salted Caramel Chocolate Magic Cake variation, trade out Homemade Caramel Sauce (page 96) for the Dark Chocolate Ganache Glaze.**

Purple Velvet Magic Cake

Makes 10 servings

Ube is a purple yam popular in many Filipino desserts and a new discovery for me. I was intrigued by this unusual ingredient when I saw several *ube* cakes online. The striking violet color caught my eye. Thanks to a global market, dried powdered *ube*, used in cakes, can easily be found in local Asian markets or online. Many *ube* cakes are topped with white *macapuno* (coconut preserves). These cakes remind me of red velvet cake with cream-cheese frosting, which is a holiday tradition at my house.

¼ cup ube powder (from a 4.06-ounce package)
4 large eggs, at room temperature
¾ cup granulated sugar
½ cup (1 stick) salted butter, melted
1 teaspoon vanilla extract
⅔ cup all-purpose flour

2 cups lukewarm whole milk
¾ teaspoon violet gel food coloring
½ teaspoon cream of tartar
1 recipe Sweetened Whipped Cream (page 91)

Preheat the oven to 325°F. Coat an 8-inch springform pan with baking spray or line an 8-inch cake pan with aluminum foil or parchment paper, if desired, and coat with baking spray.

Stir together the ube powder and ¾ cup water in a small saucepan; bring to a simmer over medium heat. Simmer 8 to 10 minutes, or until thickened, stirring often. Set mixture aside and let cool completely.

Separate the eggs; place the egg yolks in a mixing bowl with the sugar and beat on high speed with an electric mixer for 2 minutes, or until lemon colored. On low speed, gradually add the melted butter, cooled ube mixture, and vanilla, scraping down the sides as needed. Add the flour and mix just until flour is combined. Gradually add the milk, beating just until combined. Stir in violet food coloring. Add more, if necessary to reach desired purple hue.

If using the same mixer and beaters to beat the egg whites, wash the beaters thoroughly; place the egg whites in a separate mixing bowl.

Beat on medium speed until foamy; add the cream of tartar. Increase the speed to high and beat until the egg whites form stiff peaks, about 2 minutes. Gently whisk about one-third of the egg whites into the thin batter; gently fold the remaining egg whites in with a silicone spatula. Pour the batter in the prepared cake pan. Bake for 40 minutes, or until the center jiggles slightly when gently shaken.

Let cool completely on a wire rack, about 1 hour. Cover and refrigerate at least 2 hours to chill. If using a springform pan, remove sides and bottom of pan; otherwise, remove the cake from the pan using aluminum foil as handles. Remove foil and transfer the cake to a serving plate. Spread Sweetened Whipped Cream over the top of the cake.

Note: **You can deepen the purple hue of the cake by adding a drop or two of red food coloring. A combination of liquid blue and red food coloring can also be used in place of violet gel food coloring.**

Strawberry Magic Cheesecake

Makes 10 servings

The crust is not a must. The graham cracker crust makes this cake look more like a traditional cheese- cake with a magic cake surprise inside when you slice into it. It can be made without the graham cracker crust, reducing baking time by about 5 minutes.

CRUST
1⅓ cups graham cracker crumbs
2 tablespoons granulated sugar
⅓ cup salted butter, melted
CAKE
4 large eggs, at room temperature
¾ cup granulated sugar
½ cup (1 stick) salted butter, melted
1 teaspoon vanilla extract

½ (8-ounce) package cream cheese
¾ cup all-purpose flour
2 cups lukewarm whole milk
½ teaspoon cream of tartar
1 recipe Sweetened Whipped Cream (page 91)
6 ounces fresh strawberries, sliced (about 1½ cups sliced)
¼ cup strawberry jelly, melted

Preheat oven to 325°F. Coat a 9-inch springform pan with baking spray or line a 9-inch cake pan with aluminum foil, allowing 2 inches of overhang around the sides, and coat with baking spray.

CRUST
Stir together the graham cracker crumbs with the sugar and butter for the crust; press the crumb mixture into the bottom and ¾ inch up the sides of the pan. Bake for 8 minutes, or until set. (Crust will not be browned.) Let cool completely on a wire rack.

CAKE
Separate the eggs; place the egg yolks in a mixing bowl with the sugar and beat on high speed with an electric mixer for 2 minutes, or until lemon colored. On low speed, gradually add the melted butter and vanilla, scraping down sides as needed.

Place the cream cheese in a small microwave-safe bowl and microwave on HIGH for 30 seconds; add to egg yolk mixture. Beat on medium speed until cream cheese is combined. On low speed, add the flour and mix just until flour is combined. Gradually add the milk, beating just until combined.

If using the same mixer and beaters to beat the egg whites, wash the beaters thoroughly; place the egg whites in a separate mixing bowl. Beat on medium speed until foamy; add cream of tartar. Increase the speed to high and beat until the egg whites form stiff peaks, about 2 minutes. Gently whisk about one-third of the egg whites into the thin batter; gently fold the remaining egg whites in with a silicone spatula. Pour the batter into the cooled crust. Bake for 40 minutes, or until the center jiggles slightly when gently shaken.

Let cool completely on a wire rack, about 1 hour. Cover and refrigerate at least 2 hours to chill. If using a springform pan, remove sides and bottom of pan; otherwise, remove the cake from the pan using aluminum foil as handles. Remove foil and transfer the cake to a serving plate. Spread whipped cream over the top of the cake and arrange strawberries. Drizzle with melted strawberry jelly.

Note: **For a special occasion, dip whole strawberries halfway in melted dark chocolate then drizzle with melted white chocolate. Let them dry on parchment paper. Pile the chocolate-covered strawberries in the middle of the cake.**

Cardamom Sweet Potato Magic Cake with Chantilly Cream

Makes 10 servings

I prefer the roasted flavor of baked sweet potatoes to boiled sweet potatoes. Boiled potatoes also tend to retain water that could water down the custard. In the South, the holidays are not complete without a sweet potato pie. If it won't cause a family feud, try tweaking the tradition and serve Cardamom Sweet Potato Magic Cake. I think your family will be pleasantly surprised. Chantilly Cream is basically sweetened cream with either bourbon or vanilla added.

1 medium sweet potato
4 large eggs, at room temperature
¾ cup granulated sugar
½ cup (1 stick) salted butter, melted
1 teaspoon vanilla extract
¾ cup all-purpose flour
1 teaspoon ground cardamom or cinnamon

1 (12-ounce) can evaporated milk
¼ cup lukewarm whole milk
½ teaspoon cream of tartar
1 recipe Chantilly Cream (page 91)
⅛ teaspoon ground cardamom or cinnamon, for garnish

Preheat oven to 400°F. Place sweet potato on a small baking sheet lined with aluminum foil. (Go ahead and throw a few more sweet potatoes in the oven since you are already heating it up and have roasted sweet potatoes for dinner.) Bake 45 minutes, or until very soft. Cool to room temperature. Remove skin and mash sweet potato well. Measure 1 cup mashed sweet potato.

Reduce oven to 325°F. Coat a 9-inch springform pan with baking spray or line a 9-inch cake pan with aluminum foil; coat with baking spray.

Separate the eggs; place the egg yolks in a mixing bowl with the sugar and beat on high speed with an electric mixer for 2 minutes, or until lemon colored. On low speed, gradually add the melted butter, sweet potato, and vanilla, scraping down sides as needed. Add the flour and cardamom; mix just until flour is combined. Gradually add both milks, beating just until combined.

If using the same mixer and beaters to beat the egg whites, wash the beaters thoroughly; place the egg whites in a separate mixing bowl. Beat on medium speed until foamy; add cream of tartar. Increase the speed to high and beat until the egg whites form stiff peaks, about 2 minutes. Gently whisk about one-third of the egg whites into the thin batter; gently fold the remaining egg whites in with a silicone spatula. Pour the batter in the prepared cake pan. Bake for about 45 minutes, or until the center jiggles slightly when gently shaken.

Let cool completely on a wire rack, about 1 hour. Cover and refrigerate at least 2 hours to chill. If using a springform pan, remove sides and bottom of pan; otherwise, remove the cake from the pan using aluminum foil as handles. Remove foil and transfer the cake to a serving plate. Dollop with Chantilly Cream; sprinkle with ground cardamom or cinnamon.

Note: **Canned pumpkin and pumpkin pie spice can easily be substituted for sweet potato and cardamom.**

Peanut Butter and Blackberry Jam Magic Cake

Makes 9 servings

You had me at peanut butter! Anything with peanut butter in the title is at the top of my yum list. Blackberry preserves are not high on my kiddos' list, so for them, I substitute their favorite grape jam (it spreads better than jelly) and everyone's happy.

4 large eggs, at room temperature
¾ cup firmly packed light-brown sugar
¼ cup (½ stick) salted butter, melted
½ cup creamy peanut butter
1 teaspoon vanilla extract
¾ cup all-purpose flour

2 cups lukewarm whole milk
½ teaspoon cream of tartar
½ cup seedless blackberry preserves
  or your favorite jam
Fresh blackberries, for garnish

Preheat oven to 325°F. Line an 8-inch square cake pan with aluminum foil or parchment paper, allowing 2 inches of overhang around the sides; coat with baking spray.

Separate the eggs; place the egg yolks in a mixing bowl with the sugar and beat on high speed with an electric mixer for 2 minutes, or until lemon colored. On low speed, gradually add the melted butter, peanut butter, and vanilla, scraping down sides as needed. Add the flour and mix just until flour is combined. Gradually add the milk, beating just until combined.

If using the same mixer and beaters to beat the egg whites, wash the beaters thoroughly; place the egg whites in a separate mixing bowl. Beat on medium speed until foamy; add cream of tartar. Increase the speed to high and beat until the egg whites form stiff peaks, about 2 minutes. Gently whisk about one-third of the egg whites into the thin batter; gently fold the remaining egg whites in with a silicone spatula. Pour the batter in the prepared cake pan. (The pan will be almost full.) Bake for 38 to 40 minutes, or until the center jiggles slightly when gently shaken.

Let cool completely on a wire rack, about 1 hour. Cover and refrigerate at least 2 hours to chill. Remove the cake from the pan using aluminum foil as handles. Remove foil and transfer the cake to a serving plate. Spread preserves or jam evenly over the top of the cake. Garnish with blackberries.

Note: **If jelly is what you have in your pantry, microwave it on HIGH for about 20 seconds and it will spread smoothly.**

Matcha Magic Cake

Makes 9 servings

Matcha is powdered Japanese green tea leaves. Matcha is a potent source of antioxidants, and a cup of tea made with matcha contains about as much caffeine as a cup of coffee. So, what do I do on long workdays? I drink a cup of coffee with a large piece of Matcha Magic Cake for lunch and rock on!

4 large eggs, at room temperature
¾ cup granulated sugar
½ cup (1 stick) salted butter, melted
1 teaspoon vanilla extract
⅔ cup all-purpose flour
2½ tablespoons matcha tea powder

2 cups lukewarm whole milk
½ teaspoon cream of tartar
2 teaspoons unsweetened cocoa
2 teaspoons Dutch-processed cocoa
 (I use Hershey's Special Dark)
Simple plastic food-safe stencil

Preheat oven to 325°F. Line an 8-inch square cake pan with aluminum foil or parchment paper, allowing 2 inches of overhang around the sides; coat with baking spray.

Separate the eggs; place the egg yolks in a mixing bowl with the sugar and beat on high speed for 2 minutes with an electric mixer, or until lemon colored. On low speed, gradually add the melted butter and vanilla, scraping down sides as needed. Combine flour and matcha powder and mix just until combined. Gradually add the milk, beating just until combined.

If using the same mixer and beaters to beat the egg whites, wash the beaters thoroughly; place the egg whites in a separate mixing bowl. Beat on medium speed until foamy; add cream of tartar. Increase the speed to high and beat until the egg whites form stiff peaks, about 2 minutes. Gently whisk about one-third of the egg whites into the thin batter; gently fold the

remaining egg whites in with a silicone spatula.

Pour the batter in the prepared pan. Bake for 40 minutes, or until the center jiggles slightly when gently shaken.

Let cool completely on a wire rack, about 1 hour. Cover and refrigerate at least 2 hours to chill. Remove the cake from the pan using aluminum foil as handles. Remove foil and cut the cake into squares. Decorate the squares by placing the stencil on each one and sprinkling with cocoa. Use the unsweetened cocoa on half of the cake squares and the darker Dutch-processed cocoa on the other half—creating a two-toned effect. Be certain to shake excess cocoa off the stencil after each application.

Note: **Matcha is easily found online and in most higher-end supermarkets. You can make your own stencil with a piece of paper and scissors. I purchased my stencil from a craft store.**

Blueberry Blintz Magic Cake

Makes 9 servings

Cake for breakfast? Yes, please! You wouldn't think twice about eating banana bread for breakfast (which is basically cake) so try Blueberry Blintz Magic Cake when you want a change from fruit-topped pancakes for breakfast or fruit-topped cheesecake for dessert. It's also a convenient make-ahead recipe to serve overnight guests for brunch.

1 cup fresh blueberries
4 large eggs, at room temperature
¾ cup granulated sugar
½ cup (1 stick) salted butter, melted
1 teaspoon freshly grated lemon zest
1 teaspoon vanilla extract

¾ cup all-purpose flour
2 cups lukewarm whole milk
⅓ cup ricotta cheese
½ teaspoon cream of tartar
Blueberry Sauce (page 94)
Lemon zest strips, for garnish

Preheat the oven to 325°F. Line an 8-inch square cake pan with aluminum foil or parchment paper, allowing 2 inches of overhang around the sides; coat with baking spray. Place the blueberries in a single layer on the bottom of the pan.

Separate the eggs; place the egg yolks in a mixing bowl with the sugar and beat on high speed with an electric mixer for 2 minutes, or until lemon colored. On low speed, gradually add the melted butter, lemon zest, and vanilla, scraping down the sides as needed. Add the flour and mix just until flour is combined. Gradually add the milk, beating just until combined. Microwave ricotta 25 seconds in a microwave-safe bowl. Add the ricotta cheese, mixing just until combined.

If using the same mixer and beaters to beat the egg whites, wash the beaters thoroughly; place the egg whites in a separate mixing bowl. Beat on medium speed until foamy; add the cream of tartar. Increase the speed to high and beat until the egg whites form stiff peaks, about 2 minutes. Gently whisk about one-third of the egg whites into the thin batter; gently fold the remaining egg whites in with a silicone spatula. Pour the batter in the prepared cake pan. Bake for 38 to 40 minutes, or until the center jiggles slightly when gently shaken.

Let cool completely on a wire rack, about 1 hour. Cover and refrigerate at least 2 hours to chill. Remove the cake from the pan using aluminum foil as handles. Remove foil and transfer the cake to a serving plate.

Spoon Blueberry Sauce (page 94) over the cake and garnish with lemon zest strips.

Tiramisu Magic Cake

Makes 9 servings

Tiramisu is a coffee-flavored Italian dessert where sponge-cake-like ladyfinger cookies are soaked in strong coffee and rum or coffee-flavored liqueur and layered with sweetened mascarpone.

4 large eggs, at room temperature	**2 cups lukewarm whole milk**
¾ cup granulated sugar	**½ teaspoon cream of tartar**
½ cup (1 stick) salted butter, melted	**3 tablespoons strong coffee**
1½ teaspoons vanilla extract, divided	**3 tablespoons coffee-flavored liqueur**
1 (8-ounce) container mascarpone	**¼ cup confectioners' sugar**
cheese, divided	**1 cup heavy whipping cream**
¾ cup all-purpose flour	**Chocolate shavings, for garnish (see Note)**

Preheat the oven to 325°F. Line an 8-inch square cake pan with aluminum foil or parchment paper, allowing 2 inches of overhang around the sides; coat with baking spray.

Separate the eggs; place the egg yolks in a mixing bowl with the sugar and beat on high speed with an electric mixer for 2 minutes, or until lemon colored. On low speed, gradually add the melted butter and 1 teaspoon vanilla, scraping down the sides as needed. Add half of the mascarpone, mixing just until combined. Add the flour and mix just until flour is combined. Gradually add the milk, beating just until combined.

Place the egg whites in a separate mixing bowl. Beat on medium speed until foamy; add the cream of tartar. Increase the speed to high and beat until the egg whites form stiff peaks, about 2 minutes. Gently whisk about one-third of the egg whites into the thin batter; gently fold the remaining egg whites in with a silicone spatula. Pour the batter in the prepared cake pan. Bake for 38 to 40 minutes, or until the center jiggles slightly when gently shaken. Let cool completely on a wire rack, about 1 hour.

Poke holes in the sponge cake layer with a wooden skewer or a fork. Combine the coffee and liqueur, then brush or drizzle over the cake until all the coffee mixture is absorbed.

Beat the remaining mascarpone cheese, confectioners' sugar, and ½ teaspoon vanilla with a hand mixer on medium speed until smooth in a large bowl. Clean beaters and beat whipping cream in a medium bowl until stiff peaks form. Fold whipped cream into the mascarpone mixture and spread evenly over the cake. Cover and refrigerate at least 2 hours to chill.

Remove the cake from the pan using aluminum foil as handles. Remove foil and transfer the cake to a serving plate. Arrange chocolate shavings over the whipped cream mixture.

Note: **To make chocolate shavings, use a vegetable peeler to scrape a bar of semisweet chocolate.**

Caramel Apple-Cinnamon Magic Cake

Makes 10 servings

A cross between a coffee cake and a caramel flan, this eye-catching magic cake would be welcome at a casual gathering over coffee as well as a more formal dinner party. This cake is a nod to my mom's fresh apple cake she made every fall growing up in Evening Shade, Arkansas. She would always sprinkle a generous amount of brown sugar and pecans on the top, which gave it these dimples of sugary goodness. I could just eat the top layer and be a happy girl. My second favorite thing about this cake is the decadent caramel dip that can be found in the produce section of the grocery store.

1 cup caramel dip (I use Marzetti)
¾ cup peeled, finely chopped
Golden Delicious apple (about 1 small)
4 large eggs, at room temperature
¾ cup granulated sugar
½ cup (1 stick) salted butter, melted
1 teaspoon vanilla extract

¾ cup all-purpose flour
2 cups lukewarm whole milk
½ teaspoon cream of tartar
3 tablespoons light-brown sugar
3 tablespoons chopped pecans
1 teaspoon ground cinnamon
½ recipe Vanilla Icing (page 92)

Preheat the oven to 325°F. Coat an 9-inch springform pan with baking spray or line an 9-inch round cake pan with aluminum foil; coat with baking spray.

Spread the caramel dip on the bottom of the pan; sprinkle the chopped apple evenly over the caramel dip.

Separate the eggs; place the egg yolks in a mixing bowl with the sugar and beat on high speed with an electric mixer for 2 minutes, or until lemon colored. On low speed, gradually add the melted butter and vanilla, scraping down the sides as needed.

On low speed, add the flour and mix just until

flour is combined. Gradually add the milk, beating just until combined.

If using the same mixer and beaters to beat the egg whites, wash the beaters thoroughly; place the egg whites in a separate mixing bowl. Beat on medium speed until foamy; add the cream of tartar. Increase the speed to high and beat until the egg whites form stiff peaks, about 2 minutes. Gently whisk about one-third of the egg whites into the thin batter; gently fold the remaining egg whites in with a silicone spatula. Pour the batter over the apple in the prepared cake pan.

Stir together the brown sugar, pecans, and

cinnamon; sprinkle on top of the cake. Bake for 45 minutes, or until the center jiggles slightly when gently shaken. The top of the cake will have dimples like a sugar-topped coffee cake.

Let cool completely on a wire rack, about 1 hour. Cover and refrigerate at least 2 hours to chill. If using a springform pan, remove sides and bottom of pan; otherwise, remove the cake from the pan using aluminum foil as handles. Remove foil and transfer the cake to a serving plate. Drizzle with icing. Cut into slices, spooning up any caramel left behind.

Honey Walnut Magic Cake

Makes 9 servings

Sweet and simple. *Yiaourti me meli*—Greek yogurt with honey and toasted walnuts—is a popular, three-ingredient dessert that's as Greek as apple pie is American and just as delicious. The crunch of the walnut crust in this magic cake is perfectly paired with the not-so-sweet, tangy yogurt middle layer. I use raw honey from my local beekeeper. He says it tastes just like the scent of the flowers his bees visit. Take it up another notch with a small piece of honeycomb for garnish. *Opa!*

WALNUT CRUST
¾ cup finely chopped walnuts
2 tablespoons salted butter, melted
2 tablespoons granulated sugar
CAKE
4 large eggs, at room temperature
½ cup granulated sugar
½ cup (1 stick) salted butter, melted
¼ cup honey, plus more for garnish

1 teaspoon vanilla extract
¾ cup all-purpose flour
2 cups lukewarm whole milk
⅓ cup plain Greek yogurt
½ teaspoon cream of tartar
9 toasted walnut halves, for garnish
Honeycomb, for garnish
Ground cinnamon, for garnish (optional)

Preheat oven to 325°F. Line an 8-inch square cake pan with aluminum foil or parchment paper, allowing 2 inches of overhang around the sides; coat with baking spray.

WALNUT CRUST

Stir together the chopped walnuts, 2 tablespoons butter, and 2 tablespoons sugar. Firmly press the walnut mixture into the bottom of the pan. Bake for 6 minutes, or until set. Set aside and let cool slightly while preparing the cake.

CAKE

Separate the eggs; place the egg yolks in a mixing bowl with the sugar and beat on high speed with an electric mixer for 2 minutes, or until lemon colored. On low speed, gradually add the melted butter, honey, and vanilla, scraping down sides as needed. Add the flour and mix just until flour is combined. Gradually add the milk and yogurt, beating just until combined.

If using the same mixer and beaters to beat the egg whites, wash the beaters thoroughly; place the egg whites in a separate mixing bowl. Beat on medium speed until foamy; add cream of tartar. Increase the speed to high and beat until the egg whites form stiff peaks, about 2 minutes. Gently whisk about one-third of the egg whites into the thin batter; gently fold the remaining egg whites in with a silicone spatula. Pour the batter into the prepared muffin pans, filling almost full. Bake for 40 minutes, or until the center jiggles slightly when gently shaken.

Let cool completely on a wire rack, about 1 hour. Cover and refrigerate at least 2 hours to chill. Remove the cake from the pan using aluminum foil as handles. Remove foil and transfer the cake to a serving plate. Garnish with walnut halves and honeycomb and drizzle with more honey. For authentic *yiaourti* cakes, sprinkle with cinnamon.

Eggnog Magic Cake

Makes 10 servings

Rich, smooth-as-silk eggnog pairs with sweet and tangy blood oranges and pomegranate arils (seeds) to make an impressive cake for your holiday party. Blood oranges are conveniently in peak season during eggnog season, but navel oranges can also provide a stunning contrast to pomegranate. I use store-bought eggnog, but if you have a family tradition of homemade eggnog, just hold back two cups of nog before you pour it in the punch bowl. Your eggnog recipe calls for bourbon or rum? No problem: just call it Spiked Eggnog Magic Cake. Cheers!

4 large eggs, at room temperature
¾ cup granulated sugar
½ cup (1 stick) salted butter, melted
¾ cup all-purpose flour
2 cups lukewarm eggnog

½ teaspoon cream of tartar
3 small blood oranges, peeled
  and sectioned, for garnish
2 tablespoons pomegranate arils,
  for garnish

Preheat oven to 325°F. Coat an 8-inch spring-form pan with baking spray or line a 8-inch cake pan with aluminum foil; coat with baking spray.

Separate the eggs; place the egg yolks in a mixing bowl with the sugar and beat on high speed with an electric mixer for 2 minutes, or until lemon colored. On low speed, gradually add the melted butter and vanilla, scraping down sides as needed. Add the flour and mix just until flour is combined. Gradually add the milk and eggnog, beating just until combined.

If using the same mixer and beaters to beat the egg whites, wash the beaters thoroughly; place the egg whites in a separate mixing bowl. Beat on medium speed until foamy; add cream of tartar. Increase the speed to high and beat

until the egg whites form stiff peaks, about 2 minutes. Gently whisk about one-third of the egg whites into the thin batter; gently fold the remaining egg whites in with a silicone spatula. Pour the batter in the prepared cake pan. Bake for 38 to 40 minutes, or until the center jiggles slightly when gently shaken.

Let cool completely on a wire rack, about 1 hour. Cover and refrigerate at least 2 hours to chill.

If using a springform pan, remove sides and bottom of pan; otherwise remove the cake from the pan using aluminum foil as handles. Remove foil and transfer the cake to a serving plate. Arrange orange sections and pomegranate arils on the cake for garnish.

Pumpkin Magic Cake

Makes 10 servings

I use canned pumpkin but feel free to make your own pumpkin purée. Before heading out to the pumpkin patch, know that not all pumpkins are pie pumpkins. Although carving pumpkins, also called jack-o-lantern pumpkins, are edible, they tend to be stringy and not as sweet as their smaller cousin, the sugar pumpkin.

4 large eggs, at room temperature
¾ cup granulated sugar
½ cup (1 stick) salted butter, melted
1 cup canned pumpkin purée
1 teaspoon vanilla extract
¾ cup all-purpose flour

2 teaspoons pumpkin pie spice
1 (12-ounce) can evaporated milk,
½ cup lukewarm whole milk
½ teaspoon cream of tartar
2 teaspoons confectioners' sugar,
  for garnish

Preheat the oven to 325°F. Line an 9-inch square cake pan with aluminum foil or parchment paper, allowing 2 inches of overhang around the sides; coat with baking spray.

Separate the eggs; place the egg yolks in a mixing bowl with the sugar and beat on high speed with an electric mixer for 2 minutes, or until lemon colored. On low speed, gradually add the melted butter, pumpkin, and vanilla, one at a time, scraping down the sides as needed. Add the flour and pumpkin pie spice; mix just until flour is combined. Gradually add both milks, beating just until combined.

If using the same mixer and beaters to beat the egg whites, wash the beaters thoroughly; place the egg whites in a separate mixing bowl. Beat on medium speed until foamy; add the cream of

tartar. Increase the speed to high and beat until the egg whites form stiff peaks, about 2 minutes. Gently whisk about one-third of the egg whites into the thin batter; gently fold the remaining egg whites in with a silicone spatula. Pour the batter in the prepared cake pan. (The pan will be almost full.) Bake for 38 to 40 minutes, or until the center jiggles slightly when gently shaken.

Let cool completely on a wire rack, about 1 hour. Cover and refrigerate at least 2 hours to chill. Remove the cake from the pan using aluminum foil as handles. Remove foil and cut into squares. Sprinkle with confectioners' sugar for garnish.

Note: **A little extra milk is used in this recipe because the pumpkin thickens the batter.**

Turtle Magic Cake

Makes 10 servings

Dulce de leche is a caramel sauce made from caramelized milk and sugar cooked at a low tempera-
ture for a long time. I use store-bought *dulce de leche* because of the intense caramel flavor and
convenience of storing it in my pantry for spur-of-the-moment baking—which is pretty often for me.

**1 (13.4-ounce) can dulce de leche
(I use La Lechere), divided
2 cups lukewarm whole milk
4 large eggs, at room temperature
¾ cup granulated sugar
½ cup (1 stick) salted butter, melted**

**1 teaspoon vanilla extract
¾ cup all-purpose flour
½ teaspoon cream of tartar
½ recipe Ganache Glaze (page 95)
10 pecan halves, toasted
1½ tablespoons whipping cream**

Preheat oven to 325°F. Coat a 9-inch spring-form pan with baking spray or line a 9-inch cake pan with aluminum foil or parchment paper, if desired, and coat with baking spray.

Measure ½ cup dulce de leche; set aside. Spoon remaining dulce de leche into a small bowl and slowly whisk in milk until smooth.

Separate the eggs; place the egg yolks in a mixing bowl with the sugar and beat on high speed with an electric mixer for 2 minutes, or until lemon colored. On low speed, gradually add the melted butter and vanilla, scraping down sides as needed. Add the flour and mix just until flour is combined. Gradually add the milk mixture, beating just until combined.

If using the same mixer and beaters to beat the egg whites, wash the beaters thoroughly; place the egg whites in a separate mixing bowl. Beat on medium speed until foamy; add cream of tartar. Increase the speed to high and beat until the egg whites form stiff peaks, about

2 minutes. Gently whisk about one-third of the egg whites into the thin batter; gently fold the remaining egg whites in with a silicone spatula. Pour the batter in the prepared cake pan. Bake for 40 minutes, or until the center jiggles slightly when gently shaken.

Let cool completely on a wire rack, about 1 hour. Cover and refrigerate at least 2 hours to chill. If using a springform pan, remove sides and bottom of pan; otherwise, remove the cake from the pan using aluminum foil as handles. Remove foil and transfer the cake to a serving plate.

Drizzle ganache over cake, reserving 2 table-spoons. Dip pecans halfway in remaining glaze and arrange around outside edge of the cake.

In a small bowl, whisk together reserved ½ cup dulce de leche and 1½ tablespoons whipping cream; drizzle over the entire cake. Cover and refrigerate at least 30 minutes before serving for glaze to set.

Tres Leches Magic Cake

Makes 9 servings

This buttery sponge cake soaks up a sweet mixture of three milks—half-and-half, sweetened con- densed, and evaporated—while the cake is still warm. Topped with whipped cream and a hint of cinnamon, this magic cake version of a Latin American classic is a serious melt-in-your-mouth indulgence.

2 cups lukewarm half-and-half
1 (14-ounce) can sweetened condensed milk
1 (12-ounce) can evaporated milk
4 large eggs, at room temperature
½ cup granulated sugar

½ cup (1 stick) salted butter, melted
1 teaspoon vanilla extract
¾ cup all-purpose flour
½ teaspoon cream of tartar
½ recipe Sweetened Whipped Cream (page 91)
¼ teaspoon ground cinnamon

Preheat the oven to 325°F. Line an 8-inch square cake pan with aluminum foil or parchment paper, allowing 2 inches of overhang around the sides; coat with baking spray.

Stir together half-and-half, sweetened condensed milk, and evaporated milk in a medium bowl.

Separate the eggs; place the egg yolks in a mixing bowl with the sugar and beat on high speed with an electric mixer for 2 minutes, or until lemon colored. On low speed, gradually add the melted butter and vanilla, scraping down the sides as needed. Add the flour and mix just until flour is combined. Measure 2 cups of the milk mixture and gradually add it to the egg yolk mixture, beating on low speed just until combined.

If using the same mixer and beaters to beat the egg whites, wash the beaters thoroughly; place the egg whites in a separate mixing bowl. Beat on medium speed until foamy; add the cream of tartar. Increase the speed to high and beat until the egg whites form stiff peaks, about 2 minutes. Gently whisk about one-third of the egg whites into the thin batter; gently fold the remaining egg whites in with a silicone spatula. Pour the batter in the prepared cake pan. (The pan will be almost full.) Bake for 36 to 38 minutes, or until the center jiggles slightly when gently shaken.

Let stand 15 minutes. Poke holes in the sponge cake layer with a wooden skewer or a fork. Slowly pour 1 cup of the remaining milk mixture over the warm cake, a little at a time until almost all of the mixture is absorbed. It's okay if some of it spills into the bottom of the pan.

Let cool completely on a wire rack, about

45 minutes. Cover and refrigerate at least 2 hours to chill. Refrigerate the last 1 cup of milk mixture until ready to serve the cake.

Remove the cake from the pan using aluminum foil as handles. Remove foil and cut cake into squares. Place pieces of cake on serving plates with a lip or bowls. Pour chilled milk mixture over each serving, spilling onto the plate; dollop with Sweetened Whipped Cream and sprinkle with ground cinnamon.

Cappuccino Magic Cake

Makes 9 servings

Instead of serving coffee with cake, just serve Cappuccino Magic Cake and save the trouble of making coffee—this dessert has cake and coffee all rolled into one.

2 tablespoons espresso powder	**2 cups lukewarm whole milk**
4 large eggs, at room temperature	**½ teaspoon cream of tartar**
¾ cup granulated sugar	**1 recipe Sweetened Whipped Cream**
½ cup (1 stick) salted butter, melted	**(page 91)**
1 teaspoon vanilla extract	**⅓ cup chocolate-covered coffee beans,**
¾ cup all-purpose flour	**for garnish**

Preheat oven to 325°F. Line an 8-inch square cake pan with aluminum foil or parchment paper, allowing 2 inches of overhang around the sides. Stir together espresso powder and 2 teaspoons hot water in a custard cup; set aside.

Separate the eggs; place the egg yolks in a mixing bowl with the sugar and beat on high speed with an electric mixer for 2 minutes, or until lemon colored. On low speed, gradually add the melted butter, dissolved espresso, and vanilla, scraping down sides as needed. Add the flour and mix just until flour is combined. Gradually add the milk, beating just until combined.

If using the same mixer and beaters to beat

the egg whites, wash the beaters thoroughly; place the egg whites in a separate mixing bowl. Beat on medium speed until foamy; add cream of tartar. Increase the speed to high and beat until the egg whites form stiff peaks, about 2 minutes. Gently whisk about one-third of the egg whites into the thin batter; gently fold the remaining egg whites in with a silicone spatula. Pour the batter in the prepared cake pan. (The pan will be almost full.) Bake for 40 minutes, or until the center jiggles slightly when gently shaken.

Let cool completely on a wire rack, about 1 hour. Cover and refrigerate at least 2 hours to chill. Remove the cake from the pan using aluminum foil as handles. Remove foil and cut cake into squares. Dollop cake with Sweetened Whipped Cream. Garnish with chocolate-covered coffee beans.

Variation: For a mocha latte variation, stir ⅓ cup melted dark or milk chocolate into the batter and drizzle the finished cake with additional melted chocolate.

Gluten-Free Magic Cake with Glazed Fresh Fruit

Makes 10 servings

You can be confident serving this special magic cake to your friends and family if you are on a gluten-free diet. No one will ever know the difference! I tested this cake with Bob's Red Mill Gluten Free 1 to 1 Baking Flour. Not all gluten-free flours equal all-purpose flour measure for measure, so read the labels carefully.

4 large eggs, at room temperature	1 cup sliced kiwi
¾ cup granulated sugar	¾ cup sliced strawberries
½ cup (1 stick) salted butter, melted	½ cup blackberries
1 teaspoon vanilla extract	½ cup fresh navel orange sections or
¾ cup gluten-free baking flour	mandarin oranges (2 small oranges)
2 cups lukewarm whole milk	¼ cup fresh blueberries
½ teaspoon cream of tartar	3 tablespoons agave nectar or melted apple jelly

Preheat oven to 325°F. Coat an 8-inch spring-form pan with baking spray or line an 8-inch cake pan with aluminum foil; coat with baking spray.

Separate the eggs; place egg yolks in a mixing bowl with the sugar and beat on high speed with an electric mixer for 2 minutes, or until lemon colored. On low speed, gradually add the melted butter and vanilla, scraping down sides as needed. Add the flour and mix just until flour is combined. Gradually add the milk, beating just until combined.

If using the same mixer and beaters to beat the egg whites, wash the beaters thoroughly; place the egg whites in a separate mixing bowl. Beat on medium speed until foamy; add cream of tartar. Increase the speed to high and beat until the egg whites form stiff peaks, about 2 minutes. Gently whisk about one-third of the egg whites into the thin batter; gently fold the remaining egg whites in with a silicone spatula. Pour the batter in the prepared cake pan. (The pan will be almost full.) Bake for 40 to 42 minutes, or until the center jiggles slightly when gently shaken.

Let cool completely on a wire rack, about 1 hour. Cover and refrigerate at least 2 hours to chill. If using a springform pan, remove sides

and bottom of pan; otherwise, remove the cake from the pan using aluminum foil as handles. Remove foil and transfer the cake to a serving plate. Arrange fruit on top of the cake and drizzle with agave nectar.

Note: **Don't limit yourself to the fruits listed in this recipe, consider tropical fruits, such as papaya, pineapple, mango, passion fruit, star fruit, and pomegranate arils.**

Mixed Berry White Chocolate Minis

Makes 9 servings

Celebrate the Fourth of July or any occasion with these red, white, and blue mini cakes. The chilled custard centers will hit the spot on a hot summer day.

1 cup fresh raspberries, divided
1 cup fresh blueberries, divided
1¼ cups chopped white chocolate or white chocolate chips, divided
2 cups lukewarm whole milk, divided
2 large eggs, at room temperature

6 tablespoons granulated sugar
¼ cup (½ stick) salted butter, melted
½ teaspoon vanilla extract
6 tablespoons all-purpose flour
¼ teaspoon cream of tartar

Preheat the oven to 325°F. Coat 9 jumbo muffin pans or jumbo silicone cupcake liners with baking spray. If using liners, place them on a baking sheet. Arrange half of the berries in the bottom of the muffin pans or liners.

Combine ¾ cup of the white chocolate and ¼ cup milk in a small microwave-safe bowl. Microwave on HIGH for 30 seconds; stir well. Microwave 15 seconds and stir until smooth.

Separate the eggs; place the egg yolks in a

mixing bowl with the sugar and beat on high speed about 2 minutes, or until lemon colored. On low speed, gradually add the melted butter, melted white chocolate, and vanilla, scraping down the sides as needed. Add the flour and mix just until flour is combined. Gradually add the remaining 1¾ cups milk, beating just until combined, scraping down the sides as needed.

If using the same mixer and beaters to beat the egg whites, wash the beaters thoroughly;

place the egg whites in a separate mixing bowl. Beat on medium speed until foamy; add the cream of tartar. Increase the speed to high and beat until the egg whites form stiff peaks, about 2 minutes. Gently whisk about one-third of the egg whites into the thin batter; gently fold the remaining egg whites in with a silicone spatula. Pour the batter evenly in muffin pans, filling almost full. Bake for 18 minutes, or until the centers barely jiggle when gently shaken.

Let cool completely on a wire rack, about 45 minutes. Cover and refrigerate at least 1½ hours to chill.

Place remaining ½ cup white chocolate in a microwave-safe bowl or glass measuring cup. Microwave on 50 percent power for 45 seconds; stir well. Microwave 15 seconds at a time, stirring until smooth.

Run a butter knife around the outside edges of the muffin pans; carefully remove cakes from pans. Top with remaining fresh berries and drizzle with melted white chocolate.

Cookies 'n' Cream Magic Cake

Makes 10 servings

Cookies 'n' cream ice cream has been named the number-one flavor on many top-ten lists. That's not surprising because a certain cream-filled chocolate cookie is the world's best-selling cookie. So, without further ado, here's a magic-cake version combining these world-famous confections.

20 cream-filled chocolate sandwich cookies, divided
4 large eggs, at room temperature
¾ cup granulated sugar
½ cup (1 stick) salted butter, melted

1 teaspoon vanilla extract
¾ cup all-purpose flour
2 cups lukewarm whole milk
½ teaspoon cream of tartar
¾ cup cold whipping cream

Preheat oven to 325°F. Line a 9-inch square pan with aluminum foil or parchment paper, allowing 2 inches of overhang around the sides; coat with baking spray.

Coarsely crush 10 cookies in a zip-top plastic bag.

Separate the eggs; place the egg yolks in a mixing bowl with the sugar and beat on high speed with an electric mixer for 2 minutes, or until lemon colored. On low speed, gradually add the melted butter and vanilla, scraping down sides as needed. Add the flour and mix just until flour is combined. Gradually add the milk, beating just until combined.

If using the same mixer and beaters to beat the egg whites, wash the beaters thoroughly; place the egg whites in a separate mixing bowl. Beat on medium speed until foamy; add cream of tartar. Increase the speed to high and beat until the egg whites form stiff peaks, about 2 minutes. Gently whisk about one-third of the egg whites into the thin batter; gently fold the remaining egg whites and coarsely crushed cookies in with a silicone spatula. Bake for 36 to 38 minutes, or until the center jiggles slightly when gently shaken.

Let cool completely on a wire rack, about 1 hour. Cover and refrigerate at least 2 hours to chill.

Remove the cake from the pan using aluminum foil as handles. Remove foil and transfer the cake to a serving plate.

Place whipping cream in a deep, small bowl and beat with an electric hand mixer until stiff peaks form.

Crush 7 cookies in a zip-top plastic bag; the pieces should be a little smaller than the coarsely crushed cookies in the cake. Fold the crushed cookies into the whipped cream and spread over the top and sides of the cake, or dollop on individual servings, if you aren't serving the whole cake at once. Break remaining 3 cookies into small pieces and sprinkle on top of the cake.

Note: **Mini cream-filled chocolate cookies can also be used.**

Crème Caramel Magic Cake

Makes 10 servings

There's just something about this combination of homemade caramel and a custard-filled cake that makes me want to snuggle up near the fireplace and savor tiny bites at a time, making sure I recover every drop of rogue caramel that has found its way onto the plate. Yum!

4 large eggs, at room temperature
¾ cup granulated sugar
½ cup (1 stick) salted butter, melted
1 teaspoon vanilla extract
¾ cup all-purpose flour

1 (12-ounce) can evaporated milk
½ cup lukewarm whole milk
½ teaspoon cream of tartar
1 recipe Homemade Caramel Sauce (page 96)

Preheat oven to 325°F. Coat an 8-inch spring-form pan with baking spray or line an 8-inch round cake pan with aluminum foil; coat with baking spray.

Separate the eggs; place the egg yolks in a mixing bowl with the sugar and beat on high speed 2 minutes, or until lemon colored. On low speed, gradually add the melted butter and vanilla, scraping down sides as needed. Add the flour and mix just until flour is combined. Gradually add both milks, beating just until combined.

If using the same mixer and beaters to beat the egg whites, wash the beaters thoroughly; place the egg whites in a separate mixing bowl. Beat on medium speed until foamy; add cream of tartar. Increase the speed to high and beat

until the egg whites form stiff peaks, about 2 minutes. Gently whisk about one-third of the egg whites into the thin batter; gently fold the remaining egg whites in with a silicone spatula. Pour the batter in the prepared cake pan. Bake for 38 to 40 minutes, or until the center jiggles slightly when gently shaken.

Let cool 1 hour on a wire rack. Cover and refrigerate at least 2 hours to chill. If using a springform pan, remove sides and bottom of pan. Place a serving plate on top of the cake or cake pan, quickly flip the cake onto the plate so the bottom layer is on the top. If using foil-lined pan; remove aluminum foil. Pour the warm caramel over the chilled cake, allowing it to drip over the sides.

Meyer Lemon Magic Cake Bars

Makes 18 servings

When you make traditional lemon bars, you make enough for a party, right? I increased the volume of batter, added lemon zest, and baked it in a 13 x 9 x 2-inch baking pan so you can share with your friends. Feel free to cut servings smaller, if you want something more bite-size. Meyer lemons, a cross between a mandarin orange and a lemon, are slightly sweeter than a regular lemon. Their peak season is November through March. Any fresh citrus can be substituted for Meyer lemons. For a little more lemon tang, spread lemon curd over the top in place of powdered sugar. For a deeper yellow color, use free-range eggs.

6 large eggs, at room temperature
1 cup granulated sugar
¾ cup (1½ sticks) salted butter, melted
1½ teaspoons vanilla extract
1 cup all-purpose flour
3 cups lukewarm whole milk

1 tablespoon freshly grated Meyer lemon zest (from about 2 lemons), plus more for garnish
½ cup freshly squeezed Meyer lemon juice (about 3 lemons)
¾ teaspoon cream of tartar
2 teaspoons confectioners' sugar

Preheat the oven to 325°F. Line a 13 x 9 x 2-inch baking pan with aluminum foil or parchment paper, allowing 2 inches of overhang around the sides; coat with baking spray.

Separate the eggs; place the egg yolks in a large mixing bowl with the sugar and beat on high speed with an electric mixer for 2 minutes, or until lemon colored. On low speed, gradually add the melted butter and vanilla, scraping down the sides as needed. Add the flour and mix just until flour is combined. Gradually add the milk, lemon zest, and lemon juice, beating just until combined.

If using the same mixer and beaters to beat the egg whites, wash the beaters thoroughly; place the egg whites in a separate large mixing bowl. Beat on medium speed until foamy; add the cream of tartar. Increase the speed to high and beat until the egg whites form stiff peaks, about 2 minutes. Gently whisk about one-third of the egg whites into the thin batter; gently fold the remaining egg whites in with a silicone spatula. Pour the batter in the prepared cake pan. Bake for 30 minutes, or until the center barely jiggles when gently shaken.

Let cool completely on a wire rack, about 1 hour. Cover and refrigerate at least 2 hours to chill. Remove the cake from the pan using aluminum foil as handles. Remove foil and sprinkle with confectioners' sugar and lemon zest.

Variation: Lemon-Raspberry Magic Cake Bites look just like fancy petit fours. Spread ½ cup seedless raspberry jam on top of the cake just to the edges. Using an electric knife for precise cutting, cut the cake into 1-inch pieces and place in paper candy liners. Garnish with strips of lemon zest and fresh raspberries.

Note: **This cake requires less time to bake because the acid in the lemon juice starts "cooking" or denaturing the proteins of the eggs immediately.**

Apricot and Candied Ginger Magic Cake

Makes 9 servings

Apricot and ginger is a flavor marriage you see across the board in recipes from preserves to cocktails, glazes, and pan-seared pork. I especially like how it flavors the custard in this magic cake with the slight bite of ginger, while the soft apricots settle on the bottom layer, creating a chewy blondie-like texture.

6 ounces dried apricots
4 large eggs, at room temperature
¾ cup granulated sugar
½ cup (1 stick) salted butter, melted
1 teaspoon vanilla extract
½ cup all-purpose flour
¼ cup almond flour or ground blanched almonds

2 cups lukewarm whole milk
2 tablespoons chopped candied ginger
½ teaspoon cream of tartar
2 tablespoons sliced natural almonds, toasted
¼ cup apricot preserves
2 teaspoons turbinado sugar, for garnish (optional)

Preheat oven to 325°F. Line an 8-inch square cake pan with aluminum foil or parchment paper, allowing 2 inches of overhang around the sides; coat with baking spray.

Pour 1 cup boiling water over apricots in a small bowl; let stand 10 minutes.

Separate the eggs; place the egg yolks in a mixing bowl with the sugar and beat on high speed with an electric mixer for 2 minutes, or until lemon colored. On low speed, gradually add the melted butter and vanilla, scraping down sides as needed. Add the flours and mix just until flours are combined. Gradually add the milk, beating just until combined.

Drain the apricots and pat dry with paper towels. Coarsely chop the apricots. Arrange the apricots and ginger in a single layer in the bottom of the prepared pan.

If using the same mixer and beaters to beat the egg whites, wash the beaters thoroughly; place the egg whites in a separate mixing bowl. Beat on medium speed until foamy; add cream of tartar.

Increase the speed to high and beat until the egg whites form stiff peaks, about 2 minutes. Gently whisk about one-third of the egg whites into the thin batter; gently fold the remaining egg whites in with a silicone spatula. Pour the batter over the apricots and ginger. Bake for 40 minutes, or until the center jiggles slightly when gently shaken.

Let cool completely on a wire rack, about 1 hour. Cover and refrigerate at least 2 hours to chill. Remove the cake from the pan using aluminum foil as handles. Remove foil and transfer the cake to a serving plate.

Place the preserves in small microwave-safe dish and microwave 20 seconds or until melted. Sprinkle the cake with almonds and drizzle with the melted preserves. Sprinkle with turbinado sugar, if desired.

Note: **One cup sliced, fresh apricots can be substituted for rehydrated dried apricots when they are in season, which is from May to August in North America.**

S'mores Magic Cake Bars

Makes 12 servings

I have countless memories of making s'mores with fire-roasted marshmallows, graham crackers, and milk chocolate with my children. If I had my druthers, I would always choose dark chocolate over milk chocolate—so I did just that in this magic-cake rendition of s'mores. Don't wait until your next campfire to serve these ooey-gooey treats.

3½ graham cracker rectangles
4 large eggs, at room temperature
¾ cup granulated sugar
½ cup (1 stick) salted butter, melted
1 teaspoon vanilla extract
½ cup all-purpose flour
¼ cup unsweetened cocoa

1 cup dark chocolate chips
  (53 to 60% cacao)
2¼ cups lukewarm whole milk, divided
½ teaspoon cream of tartar
1½ cups mini marshmallows
1 recipe Dark Chocolate Ganache Glaze
  (page 95)

Preheat the oven to 325°F. Line a 9-inch square pan with aluminum foil or parchment, allowing 2 inches of overhang around the sides; coat with baking spray.

Place graham crackers in bottom of pan, breaking crackers to fit.

Separate the eggs; place the egg yolks in a mixing bowl with the sugar and beat on high speed with an electric mixer for 2 minutes, or until lemon colored. On low speed, gradually add the melted butter and vanilla, scraping down the sides as needed. Add the flour and cocoa; mix just until flour and cocoa are combined.

Combine chocolate chips and ½ cup of the milk in a small microwave-safe bowl; microwave on HIGH 45 seconds. Stir the mixture gently 2 or 3 times. Microwave on HIGH 25 seconds and stir until mixture is smooth. On low speed, gradually

add the chocolate mixture and remaining milk, beating just until combined.

If using the same mixer and beaters to beat the egg whites, wash the beaters thoroughly; place the egg whites in a separate mixing bowl. Beat on medium speed until foamy; add the cream of tartar. Increase the speed to high and beat until the egg whites form stiff peaks, about 2 minutes. Gently whisk about one-third of the egg whites into the thin batter; gently fold the remaining egg whites in with a silicone spatula. Pour the batter in the prepared cake pan. Bake for 35 minutes, or until the center barely jiggles when gently shaken. Immediately distribute marshmallows in a single layer on top of the cake. Place a large piece of aluminum foil loosely over cake; tent it so that it does not touch the marshmallows. Let stand 15 minutes.

This will slightly melt the marshmallows onto the cake. Let cool completely on a wire rack, about 45 minutes. Cover and refrigerate at least 2 hours to chill.

Remove the cake from the pan using aluminum foil as handles; remove foil. Toast the marshmallows with a kitchen torch; drizzle with Dark Chocolate Ganache Glaze. Let stand or chill at least 30 minutes for the ganache to set. Cut into bars.

Note: **If you don't own a kitchen torch, place the cake on the highest rack under the broiler for 1 minute or just until toasted. Watch it closely, as the marshmallows can go from toasted to burned very quickly.**

Coconut-Chocolate Magic Cake Bars

Makes 12 servings

Chocolate glaze drizzled over pillow-soft cake, a layer of creamy coconut-flavored custard, and a layer of chewy, flaked coconut on the bottom is reminiscent of one of my favorite candy bars. Sprinkle toasted almonds on top for a takeoff on another similar candy bar. Remember: canned coconut milk is for cooking; refrigerated coconut milk is for drinking.

4 large eggs, at room temperature
½ cup granulated sugar
½ cup (1 stick) salted butter, melted
⅛ teaspoon coconut extract
¾ cup all-purpose flour
1 (14-ounce) can sweetened condensed milk

½ cup lukewarm whole milk
½ cup canned coconut milk
1 cup sweetened flaked coconut
½ teaspoon cream of tartar
½ recipe Ganache Glaze (page 95)

Preheat oven to 325°F. Line an 8-inch square pan with aluminum foil or parchment paper, allowing 2 inches of overhang around the sides; coat with baking spray.

Separate the eggs; place the egg yolks in a mixing bowl with the sugar and beat on high speed with an electric mixer for 2 minutes, or until lemon colored. On low speed, gradually add the melted butter and coconut extract, scraping down sides as needed. Add the flour and mix just until flour is combined. Gradually add the milks, beating just until combined. Stir in coconut.

If using the same mixer and beaters to beat the egg whites, wash the beaters thoroughly; place the egg whites in a separate mixing bowl. Beat on medium speed until foamy; add cream of tartar. Increase the speed to high and beat until the egg whites form stiff peaks, about 2 minutes. Gently whisk about one-third of the egg whites into the thin batter; gently fold the remaining egg whites in with a silicone spatula. Pour the batter in the prepared cake pan. Bake for 35 minutes, or until the center jiggles slightly when gently shaken.

Let cool completely on a wire rack, about 1 hour. Cover and refrigerate at least 2 hours to chill. Remove the cake from the pan using foil as handles. Pour the Ganache Glaze evenly over the cake, allowing it to drip over the sides. Let stand or chill at least 30 minutes for the ganache to set. Cut into bars.

Note: **A little extra milk is added to this recipe because the coconut and sweetened condensed milk thickens the batter.**

Maple Bacon Magic Cupcakes

Makes 9 servings

Don't skimp on the maple syrup for this "dessert for breakfast/breakfast for dessert" recipe. In the photo, I'm using real maple syrup, which my brother and sister-in-law brought back from Vermont on a visit to New England. If I close my eyes, I can almost see the fall colors of the maple trees with every bite—well, not really, but it's that good.

4 large eggs, at room temperature
½ cup firmly packed light-brown sugar
½ cup (1 stick) salted butter, melted
¼ cup maple syrup, plus more for garnish
1 teaspoon vanilla extract

¾ cup all-purpose flour
2 cups lukewarm whole milk
½ teaspoon cream of tartar
5 slices applewood smoked bacon
1 recipe Maple Whipped Cream (page 91)

Preheat oven to 325°F. Coat 9 jumbo muffin pans or jumbo silicone cupcake liners with baking spray. If using liners, place them on a baking sheet.

Separate the eggs; place the egg yolks in a mixing bowl with the sugar and beat on high speed with an electric mixer for 2 minutes, or until lemon colored. On low speed, gradually add the melted butter, syrup, and vanilla, scraping down sides as needed. Add the flour and mix just until flour is combined. Gradually add the milk, beating just until combined.

If using the same mixer and beaters to beat the egg whites, wash the beaters thoroughly; place the egg whites in a separate mixing bowl. Beat on medium speed until foamy; add cream of tartar. Increase the speed to high and beat until the egg whites form stiff peaks, about 2

minutes. Gently whisk about one-third of the egg whites into the thin batter; gently fold the remaining egg whites in with a silicone spatula. Pour the batter in the muffin pans or liners. Bake for 18 to 20 minutes, or until the centers barely jiggle when gently shaken.

Meanwhile, cook bacon in a medium skillet over medium heat 8 minutes or until crisp, turning once after 5 minutes. Drain the bacon on paper towels and break into small pieces.

Let the cake cool completely on a wire rack, about 45 minutes. Cover and refrigerate at least 1½ hours to chill. Run a butter knife around outside edges of muffin pans; carefully remove the cakes from the pans to serving plates. Dollop or pipe Maple Whipped Cream on the cakes and garnish with bacon pieces. Drizzle with more maple syrup.

Marbled Magic Cake

Makes 10 servings

Sometimes I'm in the mood for chocolate, other times I prefer vanilla: most of the time I want a little of both. That's what you get with Marbled Magic Cake: the best of both worlds.

4 large eggs, at room temperature
¾ cup granulated sugar
½ cup (1 stick) salted butter, melted
1 teaspoon vanilla extract
¾ cup all-purpose flour

2 cups lukewarm half-and-half, divided
1 cup dark chocolate chips (53 to 60% cacao)
½ teaspoon cream of tartar
¼ cup chocolate syrup

Preheat the oven to 325°F. If desired, line two 8 x 4-inch loaf pans or one 12 x 4½-inch loaf pan with aluminum foil or parchment paper, allowing 2 inches of overhang around the sides; coat with baking spray.

Separate the eggs; place the egg yolks in a mixing bowl with the sugar and beat on high speed with an electric mixer for 2 minutes, or until lemon colored. On low speed, gradually add the melted butter and vanilla, scraping down the sides as needed. Add the flour and mix just until flour is combined. Gradually add 1¾ cups half-and-half, beating just until combined.

Divide the batter into two bowls: 2 cups in one bowl and 2 cups in the second bowl. Combine chocolate chips and remaining ¼ cup half-and-half in a small bowl; microwave on HIGH for 45 seconds. Stir well and microwave again for 15 seconds, stirring until smooth. Whisk chocolate mixture into one of the bowls until smooth.

If using the same mixer and beaters to beat the egg whites, wash the beaters thoroughly; place the egg whites in a separate mixing bowl. Beat on medium speed until foamy; add the cream of tartar. Increase the speed to high and beat until the egg whites form stiff peaks, about 2 minutes. Gently fold about half of the egg whites into the plain batter with a silicone spatula. Fold the remaining egg whites into the chocolate batter.

Pour the chocolate batter evenly into the prepared pans. Pour the plain batter over the chocolate batter with a back-and-forth motion. Run a table knife down and up through the center of the batter to create a marbled design on top. Do not stir the batter. Bake 8 x 4-inch loaves for 25 minutes or a 12 x 4½-inch loaf for 42 minutes, or until the center jiggles slightly when gently shaken.

Let cool completely on a wire rack, about 1 hour. Cover and refrigerate at least 2 hours to chill. Transfer the loaves to serving plates and

remove the cake from the pan using aluminum foil as handles. Remove foil. To remove loaves from the pans if you don't line them, loosen edges of loaves by running a table knife around the edges; place a large plate on top of the loaf pan; flip the pan over so loaf releases on the plate. Gently turn loaves over to reveal the marbled top. Cut loaves into slices and drizzle with chocolate syrup.

OVER THE TOP

Frostings, Glazes, & Toppings

Six-Minute Frosting

Makes 1¾ cups

Only one egg white is needed for this recipe, reducing the cooking time from the traditional 7 minutes to 6 for this marshmallow-like frosting.

¾ cup granulated sugar
1 large egg white, at room temperature
1 tablespoon light corn syrup
½ teaspoon vanilla extract

Stir together the first 3 ingredients and 2½ tablespoons water in a small, deep, and heat-proof bowl; beat on low speed with an electric mixer until foamy. Pour enough water in a small saucepan to cover the bottom but not touching the bowl; bring to a boil. Place the bowl of sugar mixture over the saucepan. Reduce heat so water just simmers.

    Beat on high speed for 6 minutes, or until stiff peaks form. Remove from heat and mix in vanilla. Use immediately because it starts to firm up quickly.

Sweetened Whipped Cream

Makes 2 cups

Why real whipped cream versus nondairy whipped topping? Because it's *real* and it's so easy and quick to make. You can't beat the flavor and texture of this two-ingredient concoction for almost anything where you want to add a dollop of yum!

1 cup cold heavy whipping cream
2 tablespoons superfine or granulated sugar

Beat whipping cream and sugar with an electric mixer in a medium-size mixing bowl on high speed about 1 minute or until stiff peaks form. Be careful not to overbeat the cream or you'll have curdled butter.

Note: **If you do overbeat the cream, gently stir in 1 to 2 tablespoons whipping cream. For best results, chill mixing bowl and beaters before using.**

Variations:

CHANTILLY CREAM: Add 1 to 2 tablespoons bourbon or 1 teaspoon vanilla extract.

MAPLE WHIPPED CREAM: Substitute 2 tablespoons maple syrup for granulated sugar.

Vanilla Icing

Makes ¾ cup

Icing versus frosting. What's the difference? Icing is thinner, typically doesn't have butter or cream, has a glossy shine, and is used for coating and drizzling. Frosting, on the other hand, is thick and fluffy, has a butter, cream, or shortening base, and is often used to frost entire cakes or tops of cupcakes. Generously pour Vanilla Icing on your magic cakes and reel in your guests as they scrape up every drop that pools onto the cake platter. Regular vanilla is perfectly fine to use but only clear vanilla will give you the snowy-white color.

2 cups confectioners' sugar
3 tablespoons whole milk
½ teaspoon clear or regular vanilla extract

Combine confectioners' sugar, milk, and vanilla in a small bowl, stirring until smooth.

Note: **Clear vanilla can be found in most grocery or discount stores where cake-decorating supplies are sold. I prefer the flavor of real vanilla extract.**

Toffee Sauce

Makes 1¼ cups

Make a double batch of this buttery sauce to put in half-pint mason jars for gift giving.
Store any leftovers in the refrigerator in an airtight container to reheat later and serve over ice cream.

½ cup (1 stick) salted butter
1 cup firmly packed dark-brown sugar
½ cup whipping cream
1 teaspoon vanilla extract

Cook the butter and brown sugar in a small saucepan over medium heat, stirring often, or until it comes to a boil. Boil 1 minute. Stir in whipping cream and vanilla.

Blueberry Sauce

Makes 2 cups

Serve with Blueberry Blintz Magic Cake (page 50). Enjoy any leftover warm Blueberry Sauce over vanilla ice cream, on pancakes and waffles, or stirred into yogurt and granola.

2 cups fresh or frozen blueberries
¼ cup granulated sugar
½ teaspoon vanilla extract
1½ teaspoons cornstarch

Stir together all of the ingredients with ¼ cup water in a small saucepan; bring the mixture to a boil, stirring constantly, and cook until it is slightly thickened, 4 to 5 minutes.

Ganache Glaze

Makes 1½ cups

Drizzle, pour, or spoon this rich, smooth, glossy glaze over your favorite cakes. It can also be used as a sauce or filling. The consistency depends on the temperature of the Ganache Glaze—the cooler the glaze, the thicker it becomes. It can also be whipped when completely cool and then piped in a pastry bag for a decorative look on cakes and mini cakes.

1¼ cups semisweet chocolate chips
⅔ cup whipping cream

Combine chocolate chips and whipping cream in a 2-cup microwave-safe measuring cup; microwave on HIGH for 1 minute. Let stand 30 seconds. Stir chocolate chips and whipping cream together until smooth.

Note: **Ganache Glaze can also be made on the stove by heating the whipping cream first and then adding the chocolate, but it works just as well in the microwave, and I like having it ready to pour in a measuring cup with a spout.**

Variation:
DARK CHOCOLATE GANACHE GLAZE:
Substitute dark chocolate chips for semisweet chips.

Homemade Caramel Sauce

Makes ⅔ cup

There's no substitute for the deep, complex flavor caramelized sugar creates in this simple sauce. The cream will send up a cloud of steam when added to the hot caramelized sugar but keep stirring: it fades quickly.

½ cup granulated sugar
⅓ cup heavy whipping cream

Combine the sugar and ¼ cup water in a medium-size, heavy-bottomed saucepan. Cook over medium heat, stirring occasionally, just until sugar dissolves. Cook, without stirring, 8 to 10 minutes, or until the mixture is an amber color. Swirl the pan toward the end of cooking for even color distribution, being careful not to swirl up the sides of the pan where sugar might have crystallized. Add whipping cream, stirring quickly until sugar mixture combines with cream.

CURTAIN CALL

When the curtain closes at the end of a production, the cast reappears so the audience can applaud their hard work and talented performance. I have many people to thank for their role in this sweet production.

First, I am grateful for my husband, Scott, for his willingness to stop everything at any given moment throughout the recipe development, testing, editing, and photography to help with the dishes and laundry, for all the times I asked him to stop and pick up yet another gallon of milk on his way home from work, and for making me laugh every day for the past twenty-two years. My daughter, Corinne, for bringing home her sweet tooth, not her laundry, on her breaks from college. My son, Grayson, for never hesitating to sample cake for breakfast, lunch, or dinner as the need arose. I applaud my talented photographer and friend, Becky Luigart-Stayner: her attention to detail enhanced every photograph. Jan Gautro, my prop stylist, for being so cheerful even when the workday turned into the evening. You both made my job as the food stylist "a piece of cake." Julia Dowling Rutland for having the confidence in me to recommend me for developing the recipes. Martha Hopkins, my agent with Terrace Partners, for patiently answering my plethora of questions and guiding me on this journey. Kristen Green Wiewora, editor, for trusting me to create these recipes and for her words of encouragement. Amanda Richmond, designer, for her creativity and vision for the design of *Magic Cakes*. Amber Morris, project editor, for her patience with last minute changes and *the entire team at Running Press*.

Finally, my parents, Jim and Eva Royal, who taught me at an early age that whatever you do in life, do it to the best of your ability. I hope when you read my cookbook you will say, "That's real nice."

INDEX

Note: Page references in *italics* indicate photographs.

A

Almonds
Apricot and Candied Ginger Magic Cake, 78–79
Cranberry-Orange Magic Cake, *32, 33*
Aluminum foil, lining pans with, 15
Apple, Caramel, –Cinnamon Magic Cake, *54, 55*–56
Apricot and Candied Ginger Magic Cake, 78–79

B

Bacon Maple Magic Cupcakes, *84, 85*
Banana Pudding Magic Cake, 30, *31*
Bars, Magic Cake
Coconut-Chocolate, 82–83
Lemon-Raspberry Magic Cake Bites, 78
Meyer Lemon, *76, 77*–78
S'mores, 80–82, *81*
Blackberry(ies)
Gluten-Free Magic Cake with Glazed Fresh Fruit, 68–70, *69*
Jam and Peanut Butter Magic Cake, 46, *47*
Blueberry(ies)
Blintz Magic Cake, 50, *51*
Gluten-Free Magic Cake with Glazed Fresh Fruit, 68–70, *69*
Mixed Berry White Chocolate Minis, 70–71
Sauce, 94
Bourbon
Chantilly Cream, 91

Butter

melting, 12
salted *versus* unsalted, 11

C

Cake pans, square or round, 13
Cake sparklers
about, 34
Magical Confetti Birthday Cake, 34, *35*
Cappuccino Magic Cake, 66–67
Caramel
Apple–Cinnamon Magic Cake, *54,* 55–56
Chocolate Magic Cake, Salted, 40
Crème Caramel Magic Cake, 74, *75*
Sauce, Homemade, 96
Turtle Magic Cake, 62, *63*
Cardamom Sweet Potato Magic Cake with Chantilly Cream, 44–45
Ceramic pans, note about, 16
Chantilly Cream, 91
Cheese
Blueberry Blintz Magic Cake, 50, *51*
Strawberry Magic Cheesecake, *42,* 43–44
Tiramisu Magic Cake, 52, *53*
Cheesecake, Strawberry Magic, *42,* 43–44
Chocolate
-Coconut Magic Cake Bars, 82–83
Cookies 'n' Cream Magic Cake, *72, 73*
creating a German chocolate magic cake, 18
Dark, Ganache Glaze, 95
Dark, Salted, Magic Cake, 38–40, *39*
-dipped strawberries, preparing, 44
Ganache Glaze, 95

Magic Cake, *22*, 23
Marbled Magic Cakes, 86–88, *87*
Salted Caramel, Magic Cake, 40
S'mores Magic Cake Bars, 80–82, *81*
Turtle Magic Cake, 62, *63*
White, Mixed Berry Minis, 70–71
Coconut
  -Chocolate Magic Cake Bars, 82–83
  Cream Magic Cake, *28*, 29
  creating a German chocolate magic
    cake with, 18
  Key Lime Magic Cake, 24–25
Coffee
  Cappuccino Magic Cake, 66–67
  Tiramisu Magic Cake, 52, *53*
Cookies 'n' Cream Magic Cake, *72*, 73
Cranberry-Orange Magic Cake, *32*, 33
Crème Caramel Magic Cake, 74, *75*
Cupcakes, Maple Bacon Magic, *84*, 85
Curd, Orange, Gingerbread Magic Cake
  with, 26–27

D
Dates
  Magic Sticky Toffee Puddings, *36*, 37
Dulce de leche
  Turtle Magic Cake, 62, *63*

E
Eggnog Magic Cake, 58, *59*
Eggs
  beating with sugar, 16–17
  bringing to room temperature, 11
  for recipes, 10–11
  whipping whites of, 10–11, 16

Electric mixers, 16–17
Equipment
  baking pans, 13–16
  electric mixer, 16–17

F
Flour, measuring, 12
Frosting, Six-Minute, 90
Fruit. *See also specific fruits*
  Glazed Fresh, Gluten-Free Magic Cake
    with, 68–70, *69*

G
Ganache Glaze, 95
Ganache Glaze, Dark Chocolate, 95
Ginger
  Candied, and Apricot Magic Cake, 78–79
  Gingerbread Magic Cake with Orange
    Curd, 26–27
Glass pans, note about, 16
Glazes
  Dark Chocolate Ganache, 95
  Ganache, 95
Gluten-Free Magic Cake with Glazed
  Fresh Fruit, 68–70, *69*
Graham crackers
  S'mores Magic Cake Bars, 80–82, *81*
  Strawberry Magic Cheesecake, *42*, 43–44

H
Hand mixers, 16
Honey Walnut Magic Cake, 56–57

I
Icing, Vanilla, 92

Ingredients
    butter, 11–12
    eggs, 10–11
    flour, 12
    milk, 12–13
    room temperature, 9–10
    sugar, 12

K
Key Lime Magic Cake, 24–25
Kiwi
    Gluten-Free Magic Cake with Glazed Fresh
      Fruit, 68–70, *69*

L
Lemon
    Meyer, Magic Cake Bars, *76*, 77–78
    -Raspberry Magic Cake Bites, 78
Lime(s)
    juicing, tip for, 25
    Key, Magic Cake, 24–25

M
Magical Confetti Birthday Cake, 34, *35*
Magic Cake Bars
    Coconut-Chocolate, 82–83
    Lemon-Raspberry Magic Cake Bites, 78
    Meyer Lemon, *76*, 77–78
    S'mores, 80–82, *81*
Magic Cakes
    Apricot and Candied Ginger, 78–79
    baking times, 17
    Banana Pudding, 30, *31*
    Blueberry Blintz, 50, *51*
    Cappuccino, 66–67

Caramel Apple–Cinnamon, *54*, 55–56
Cardamom Sweet Potato, with Chantilly
    Cream, 44–45
Chocolate, *22*, 23
Coconut Cream, *28*, 29
Cookies 'n' Cream, *72*, 73
Cranberry-Orange, *32*, 33
creating a German chocolate cake, 18
Crème Caramel, 74, *75*
designing your own, 18
Eggnog, 58, *59*
Gingerbread, with Orange Curd, 26–27
Gluten-Free, with Glazed Fresh Fruit,
    68–70, *69*
Honey Walnut, 56–57
ingredients for, 9–13
Key Lime, 24–25
kitchen equipment for, 13–17
Magical Confetti Birthday Cake, 34, *35*
Magic Sticky Toffee Puddings, *36*, 37
Maple Bacon Magic Cupcakes, *84*, 85
Marbled, 86–88, *87*
Matcha, *48*, 49
Mixed Berry White Chocolate Minis, 70–71
Peanut Butter and Blackberry Jam, 46, *47*
preparing, 8–9
Pumpkin, *60*, 61
Purple Velvet, 40–41
Salted Caramel Chocolate, 40
Salted Dark Chocolate, 38–40, *39*
storing, 17
Strawberry Magic Cheesecake, *42*, 43–44
tests for doneness, 17
Tiramisu, 52, *53*
Tres Leches, *64*, 65–66

MAGIC CAKES

Turtle, 62, *63*
Vanilla, 20, *21*
Maple
    Bacon Magic Cupcakes, *84*, 85
    Whipped Cream, 91
Marbled Magic Cakes, 86–88, *87*
Marshmallows
    S'mores Magic Cake Bars, 80–82, *81*
Matcha
    buying, 49
    Magic Cake, *48*, 49
Meyer Lemon Magic Cake Bars, *76*, 77–78
Milk
    bringing to room temperature, 13
    canned coconut, 13
    evaporated, 12–13
    for recipes, 12–13
    whole, 12
Mixed Berry White Chocolate Minis, 70–71
Mixers, electric, 16–17

N
Nuts
    Apricot and Candied Ginger Magic Cake,
        78–79
    Caramel Apple–Cinnamon Magic Cake,
        54, 55–56
    Cranberry-Orange Magic Cake, *32*, 33
    creating a German chocolate magic cake
        with, 18
    Honey Walnut Magic Cake, 56–57
    Turtle Magic Cake, 62, *63*

O
Orange(s)
    Curd, Gingerbread Magic Cake with, 26–27
    Eggnog Magic Cake, 58, *59*
    Gluten-Free Magic Cake with Glazed Fresh
        Fruit, 68–70, *69*

P
Pans
    ceramic, note about, 16
    glass, note about, 16
    lining with aluminum foil, 15
    rectangular baking pans, 13
    silicone, 15–16
    springform, 13–15
    square or round cake pans, 13
Parchment paper, note about, 15
Peanut Butter and Blackberry Jam Magic
    Cake, 46, *47*
Pecans
    Caramel Apple–Cinnamon Magic Cake,
        54, 55–56
    creating a German chocolate magic
        cake with, 18
    Turtle Magic Cake, 62, *63*
Pomegranate arils
    Eggnog Magic Cake, 58, *59*
Pumpkin
    Magic Cake, *60*, 61
    using in cake recipe, 45
Purple Velvet Magic Cake, 40–41

R

Rainbow sprinkles
  Magical Confetti Birthday Cake, 34, *35*
Raspberry(ies)
  -Lemon Magic Cake Bites, 78
  Mixed Berry White Chocolate Minis, 70–71
Rectangular baking pans, 13
Red velvet magic cake, preparing, 23

S

Salted Caramel Chocolate Magic Cake, 40
Salted Dark Chocolate Magic Cake, 38–40, *39*
Sauces
  Blueberry, 94
  Caramel, Homemade, 96
  Toffee, 93
Silicone pans, 15–16
Six-Minute Frosting, 90
S'mores Magic Cake Bars, 80–82, *81*
Springform pans, 13–15
Stand mixers, 16
Stencils, making your own, 49
Sticky Toffee Puddings, Magic, *36, 37*
Strawberry(ies)
  chocolate-covered, preparing, 44
  Gluten-Free Magic Cake with Glazed
    Fresh Fruit, 68–70, *69*
  Magic Cheesecake, *42,* 43–44
Sugar
  beating eggs with, 16–17
  for cakes, 12
Sweet Potato Cardamom Magic Cake
  with Chantilly Cream, 44–45

T

Tiramisu Magic Cake, 52, *53*
Toffee Sauce, 93
Tres Leches Magic Cake, *64,* 65–66
Turtle Magic Cake, 62, *63*

U

Ube powder
  Purple Velvet Magic Cake, 40–41

V

Vanilla
  clear, buying, 92
  Icing, 92
  Magic Cake, 20, *21*

W

Walnut Honey Magic Cake, 56–57
Whipped Cream
  Chantilly Cream, 91
  Maple, 91
  overbeating, remedy for, 91
  Sweetened, 91
White Chocolate Mixed Berry Minis, 70–71